THE MAGIC
NEVER ENDS

THE MAGIC NEVER ENDS

An Oral History of the Life and Work of C. S. Lewis

JOHN RYAN DUNCAN

W PUBLISHING GROUP™

www.wpublishinggroup.com

A Division of Thomas Nelson, Inc.
www.ThomasNelson.com

Published by W Publishing Group, a Division of Thomas Nelson, Inc., P.O. Box 141000, Nashville, Tennessee 37214.

Grateful acknowledgment is extended to the following publishers for their permission in reprinting portions of C. S. Lewis's work.

From *Jack: A Life of C. S. Lewis* by George Sayer, copyright © 1994, pages 317, 410. Used by permission of Crossway Books, a division of Good News Publishers, Wheaton, Illinois 60187.

From *Mere Christianity* by C. S. Lewis © Copyright C. S. Lewis PTE, Ltd. 1942, 1943, 1944, 1952.

From *The Quotable Lewis* © 1989 Wayne Martindale and Jerry Root, Editors. Used by permission of Tyndale House Publishers, Inc. All rights reserved.

Excerpts from *Surprised by Joy: The Shape of My Early Life* by C. S. Lewis, copyright © 1956 by C. S. Lewis PTE Ltd. and renewed 1984 by Arthur Owen Barfield, reprinted by permission of Harcourt, Inc.

ISBN 0-8499-1718-2

Printed in the United States of America

01 02 03 04 05 PHX 5 4 3 2 1

To Anna Duncan—
the beautiful little girl who makes
everyone around her believe in magic.

Contents

ACKNOWLEDGMENTS

This book and the related documentary film could not have been produced without the contributions and support of colleagues and friends including David Crouse, Bob Huck, Steve Nelson, Scott Eisenstein, Cathy Ryan, Pat Hammerlund, David Barrett, Elaine Joli, Shaun Mader, Cheryl McShane, Francis Warner, Gail Standish Ward, Ryan Hankins, Peter Cousin, Jim Shaw, Randy Bobo, Peter Batchelder, Jill Keenleyside, Peter Buffett, Mary Beth Hughes, Alyce Myatt, Sandy Heberer, Stevie Ballard, Melissa Lamb Topp, Bob Kendall, Lisa Fitzwilliams, Victor Estrada, Chris Spheeris, Alison Rostankowski, Matt Slocum, Darele Heisdorf, Michael Bolger, Debra Winger, Susan Templin, Peter and Trish Fogg, and Ben Kingsley.

I give special thanks to Marjorie Mead and the staff of the Marion E. Wade Center at Wheaton College in Wheaton, Illinois, for their kindness and for their thoroughness with regard to the C. S. Lewis archives. Thanks to Holly Halverson for her editorial consultation. And it's important to note that this book would not have been possible without the research and editorial support of Patricia Ostermick. Her quiet passion for scholarly pursuit and attention to detail add significantly to everything our small company is fortunate to produce.

I'm especially grateful to those we interviewed for both the film and book, and I thank them for their time and their insights. Most of all, I thank C. S. Lewis for his lasting body of work . . . and his readers throughout the world for the inspiration they provide.

INTRODUCTION

Novelist. Children's fantasy writer. Poet. Lecturer. Radio commentator. Oxford scholar and teacher. Christian apologetic writer. A stocky, balding, nearly lifelong bachelor from the cloistered world of England's Oxford University, C. S. Lewis was a versatile, thoughtful, talented, yet humble man who just might rank among the greatest writers in the English language. Yet defining Lewis as among the greatest requires a broad view of his work. Would he qualify as a poet? Not likely. As a novelist? Perhaps not. In fact, Dabney Hart, an Atlanta-based English professor who's written and lectured extensively about C. S. Lewis said, "I think it does no disservice to him to say that he is not one of the great novelists of the twentieth century. I think he would have been the first person to say that himself."

So what was he? In what does this acclaimed man's greatness lie? Hart, like so many others who've discovered Lewis's writings during the past fifty to sixty years, understands that his success and prominence cannot be interpreted by evaluating his novels or poetry alone. The fact is that the greatness of C. S. Lewis's writing does not arise merely from his craft with words or his ingenious plot lines. It doesn't come only from his unique characters, his imagination, or the worlds he created outside the reality we all live with day to day. The greatness of C. S. Lewis's writing comes from his ability to simplify an intellectual or philosophical concept and to assist readers on a spiritual journey of their own. He did it as a novelist (in such works as *Till We Have Faces, Out of the Silent Planet,* and *That Hideous Strength*), as the author of children's fantasy literature (The Chronicles of Narnia series), as a satirist (*The Screwtape Letters*), and as the writer of numerous volumes of Christian apologetics and essays, including *Mere Christianity, The Problem of Pain, Miracles,* and *A Grief Observed.*

To measure the success of Lewis's work, one need look only at its longevity and to the passion his writing evokes among his readers, who grow in number year after year. C. S. Lewis is among those rare talents who, by defining his own spiritual path and interpreting his journey in his writings, has helped to create a life-changing opportunity for others. In this, an oral history on his life and work, I hope to share the insights and knowledge of those who knew him, as well as those who have given much of their lives to a study of his work.

———◆———

To say that the work of C. S. Lewis is popular, commercially successful, and critically unique is a classic understatement. In fact, the entire body of Lewis's work—all thirty-eight books—has *never* been out of print. Millions of readers from all walks of life, from all parts of the world, both secular and nonsecular, are not just readers of his work—they are devoted readers of his work. Recent sales statistics show that more than 200 million copies of Lewis's books have been sold worldwide and, since 1989, more than 1.5 million copies of books in The Chronicles of Narnia series have been sold annually. It's safe to say that Lewis's popularity continues to grow as more and more readers are exposed to his books. At present, there are more than 200 individual fan clubs, readers groups, and C. S. Lewis societies around the world.[1]

But it's also important to note that Lewis fans are different—different because his books touch both Christian and non-Christian readers on a *soul* level. Why? Because Lewis used his work to ask the philosophical, psychological, and moral questions that are at the core of every person's existence.

Is there a God?

If so, is there only one God?

If there is a God, then why does evil permeate our world? Why are there famine, war, overpopulation, death, and destruction?

How does belief in God help nurture happiness and fulfillment? How does faith heal and help someone overcome pain?

For many of Lewis's readers, his conversion to and understanding of his Christian faith have become a significant part of their own conversion to Christianity. Lyle Dorsett, professor of evangelism and spiritual formation at Wheaton College and Graduate School in Wheaton, Illinois, suggested, "Lewis is one of the reasons I'm a Christian. He's not the only reason. But his writings were very influential. It was also very instructive for me to read his autobiographical work, *Surprised by Joy,* and to see that our pilgrimages were somewhat similar. There was always a longing in Lewis. But there was a world-view that was naturalistic and materialistic, but yet being drawn into something that you really didn't particularly want to be drawn into. I was afraid of becoming a Christian because I was afraid I'd change. And I thought I'd never have fun again. But the opposite was true. He taught me a theology of prayer. He's the one that instructed me on the basics of faith."

Throughout his life, Lewis remained spiritually inquisitive. And he used both his fiction and nonfiction writing to develop a defense of the faith in which he came to believe. Because he wrote not as a preacher but as a teacher, his fictional work continues to reach well beyond Christian followers. In fact, many who read Lewis visit his worlds without ever knowing that he writes from a Christian perspective.

"I think that's one of his most brilliant accomplishments," said Colin Manlove, professor of English at Edinburgh University, Scotland. "C. S. Lewis was a man who had a tremendous mind and he used it to explain joys that he felt all through his life as coming from God. You can't compare him with Lawrence or Forester or Wolfe—he wasn't trying to do the same thing. You have to talk about Lewis in terms of the different aims he had, and they come down to the realization of joy, the idea of putting newness inside fiction, the idea of making Christianity believable without actually naming it—all these things. And, of course, the idea of putting together a fantasy and making a world that works. All these things are not valued in twentieth-century criticism.

"He always felt that although his fiction obviously had a moral or religious intent, that the first concern was to be true to his motives in writing," continued Manlove. "Lewis wrote as though he were a plain, ordinary, old atheist turning into a Christian."

The way Lewis posed spiritual questions in both his fiction and nonfiction writing set him apart from many writers of his or any generation. Few writers are able to place the search for God or enlightenment in a context that is equally thought-provoking and entertaining. Lewis was able to walk that fine line. His intellect and his vast knowledge of English literature and mythology helped him craft his argument and his storytelling. But it was more than that. Lewis was also able to harness the same imagination and creativity that served him as a child, and use them to explore different worlds, colorful landscapes, and multi-dimensional characters consumed by the same human frailties and temptations that besiege us all.

Because he wrote in so many different genres and styles, C. S.

Lewis was able to use his fictional writing to convey moral and ecological values that complemented the spiritual and attracted a global following. "One of the things he had to offer was multi-culturalism," said Manlove. "Practically all of Lewis's books are about getting used to and getting on with the alien, getting on with the strange. Whether it's a faun or a 'marshwiggle' or a 'green lady' who is originally innocent on a strange oceanic planet, all of these things involve getting on with those absolutely unlike oneself. In that sense, he's talking about how we accommodate ourselves to the unfamiliar, to the foreign.

"Another aspect is the sort of ecological sense that comes from Lewis—he's constantly valuing animals. And the whole of *Perelandra*, for instance, is about preserving innocence and, with it, preserving a planet that is basically full of life and variety."

Readers from any background will discover that the core of Lewis's work is about values, morality, and the battle between good and evil. Yet it was Lewis's imagination that helped to create the quality that many admire most: the open, curious mind that never stopped exploring the landscape and the ever-changing dynamics of the search for God and happiness. In that, we find a man who never stopped growing, a man who never stopped learning, a man who never hopped off the train of life believing he had all the answers. Lewis began his adolescence as an atheist, and he ended his adulthood as a devout, reflective Christian. Along the way, he became a teacher and a writer. It was Lewis's active and intellectual exploration of faith that guided him through much of his adult life, through his role as a Christian writer, through his unique and powerful friendships, and through the pain he felt at the loss of his wife.

While it is Lewis's work that is both lasting and inspired, there is an ongoing interest in who Lewis was as a man. It may surprise many to learn that much of his adulthood was defined by its simple routine. Lewis lived a quiet, communal, and uniquely provincial lifestyle that's in sharp contrast to the worlds he explored in his books. He often said he was a throwback to an earlier century. In many ways he was. He didn't drive, he rarely wore a watch, and, until late in life, his travels were limited to Ireland, England, and a brief wartime service in France. From the age of eighteen, he made Oxford his home.

When she met Lewis in person, Dabney Hart found him unassuming. "He seemed like a dear and very likable, even lovable person—someone who might have been a relative or a friend of my parents," she said. "It would never have occurred to me to react to him as someone with a great deal of charismatic appeal. He just seemed too ordinary for that."

"He had many friends," said Walter Hooper, an editor of numerous books on Lewis and, according to Hooper, an assistant to Lewis near the time of his death. "He often rejoiced when he was on a train and he could talk to an ordinary man about literature because, he thought, when you're talking to an ordinary man about Jane Austen, this man really liked her books. That's why he read them. But if you were talking to a fellow professional, you weren't sure whether he really liked them or whether he's merely writing a book about them."

Hooper added, "When I asked him to talk about the Narnia stories, he didn't talk about them as the man who wrote them. His interest was in the books themselves. I was surprised that he was so humble. I really hadn't expected it.

"I was also surprised to find that Lewis's house was so basic. There was even a hole in the floor that you had to be careful of so the chair didn't fall into it. And the food he liked couldn't have been simpler: sausages and mashed potatoes, fish and chips.

THE KILNS.

"He was humble and kind, and such a simple man. I can't imagine anyone not feeling comfortable with him," Hooper continued. "One might find his conversation very rich, but there was nothing daunting about his home or the way he lived. He was one of those fortunate people who didn't really need much to make him happy. If you had put him in a palace, he would have admired it for its beauty, but he didn't need those things."

"Lewis was, to me, a very extraordinary person," said Colin Manlove. "He was not someone whose sexual preferences, personal idiosyncrasies, faults, failures, and so forth are particularly evident. He was someone who was extremely modest, careless of appearance, someone who lived in humility and innocence. He was always seen as he presented himself, and we don't know much of what lay behind it. I don't mind. For me, it's an attraction in Lewis because I know a lot of his heart is in his books."

"He was a man of habit," said Chris Mitchell, director of the Marion E. Wade Center at Wheaton College—the world's largest repository of C. S. Lewis's scholarly writings and memorabilia. "I don't think he was the sort of guy who necessarily stood out unless you engaged him. You would never have thought of him as an Oxford don because of the way he dressed. Neat freaks would not have admired Lewis. He could be loud and boisterous but I don't know that his personality could be called eccentric. His life was filled with friends, teaching at the college, reading, and his work. And of course, walking. But he didn't take in the cinema. He didn't have a public social life. Especially in American contemporary terms, he was kind of a boring guy—which is ironic because he's anything but that in his writings."

There are many who suggest that Lewis would be embarrassed by all the attention that's placed on his lifestyle, his personality, and his relationships. Yet that hasn't stopped thousands of fans from touring his old haunts in Oxford—from pubs such as the Eagle and Child and the Trout on the river Thames to Addison's Walk behind Magdalen College, the Bodlien Library, and the University Church. Hundreds of people visit his home (called "the Kilns") each year and many include a stop at the cemetery outside Holy Trinity Church to visit his grave. While it's safe to say that Lewis's day-to-day life was mostly unremarkable, he did one thing incredibly well, and it's that for which he would no doubt like to be remembered. C. S. Lewis spent hours each day mulling ideas while walking, researching, and reading in the Bodleian Library. And then, hunched over a tablet, nib pen and inkwell at hand, Lewis had one simple goal in mind: to share his imagination, ideas, and beliefs through his writing.

Yet the man still fascinates readers worldwide, despite Lewis's own objections. Dabney Hart, who met Lewis at Cambridge while doing her doctoral work on his writing said, "Lewis believed that it is false literary criticism to concentrate on learning about the author, and learning about whether he got along with his mother, and so on. He said that when you try to find out all these features of the author's life and try to relate them to the book, it's not literary criticism; it's gossip. If you cannot understand the novel or the poem on its own, if you have to go to the author's life to find out the clues to understanding it, then there are only two possibilities. Either the author has failed to make his point in the work of art, or you lack the ability to understand it.

"There are many people who would disagree with that. There are people who love to go sifting through all the works to find little details here and there that reflect part of Lewis's own experience. Sometimes, I admit, I'm guilty of calling attention to details like that just because I know an audience enjoys them. But I'm almost ashamed of myself when I do it," said Hart, laughing.

Despite Lewis's own objection to people's knowing more about him on a personal level, it can also be argued that such details enhance the understanding of his work. Yet to know Lewis as a man is a challenge. While the basic facts of his life are well documented and the philosophical course of his life is covered in his autobiography, *Surprised by Joy,* there are few alive today who knew him intimately. His professional life was filled with lectures, books, articles, and BBC radio addresses, of which copies and transcripts remain. His interactions with his literary colleagues, the Inklings, are well noted; yet much of their time was spent in friendly comment, philosophical argument, and literary criticism. What allows us to meet C. S. Lewis today are the insights of those few people who did know Lewis as well as the in-depth analyses of his writings from scholars who have spent years studying his work.

Many of the interview insights that comprise the following chapters were compiled during the course of a television documentary production on C. S. Lewis called *The Magic Never Ends: The Life & Work of C. S. Lewis,* which is a visual companion to this book. Produced by Crouse Entertainment Group (*CrouseEntertainment.com*) and the Duncan Group (*DuncanEntertainment.com*), it can be viewed on public television in the United States and on numerous networks around the world.

As part of the production, we were granted interviews with some of the very few people still alive who knew Lewis as well as several of the world's leading scholars who have spent their lives studying his work. They include:

Douglas Gresham—minister, writer, former journalist, stepson of C. S. Lewis, and son of Joy Davidman and William Lindsay Gresham. Born in New York, Gresham spent much of his youth in Oxford, England, with his mother, his brother, David, C. S. Lewis, and Lewis's brother, Warnie.

Following his parents' divorce in 1954, Gresham went to school in Surrey, England. The next year the family moved to Headington, Oxford. After his mother died in 1960 and his father in 1962, Gresham continued to live with C. S. Lewis in their Headington Quarry home until Lewis's death in 1963.

For the next few years, Gresham studied agriculture and worked on farms, and during this time he met and fell in love with Meredith Conan-Davies. Shortly after their wedding, he and Merrie sailed for Australia. During many eventful years there, he worked as a farmer, a radio and television broadcaster, a restaurateur, and "many other things between."

Since 1973, Gresham has worked with the estate of C. S. Lewis. In 1993, the family moved to Carlow County, Ireland. Gresham and his wife, both of whom are committed Christians, have made their home into a multifaceted, nondenominational Christian House Ministry that specializes in counseling and seminar hosting.

In 1988, Gresham published his autobiographical book *Lenten Lands*, which included insights into his own relationship with C. S. Lewis and the marriage between Lewis and his mother. Gresham now works full-time for the C. S. Lewis Company, and he and his wife devote their spare time to "addressing whatever work the Lord sends them."

Walter Hooper—writer, Lewis scholar, and editor. Born and educated in North Carolina, Walter Hooper's life changed immeasurably when he relocated to Oxford, England, in the early 1960s. According to Hooper, it was during this time that he volunteered as a personal assistant to C. S. Lewis. As a temporary resident of Lewis's home, the Kilns, says Hooper, he got to know Lewis personally. He gained insights into Lewis's prolific correspondence with fans and friends and he studied his writings. Though in graduate school in the United States when Lewis died, Hooper later returned to Oxford where he's become the editor of several collections of Lewis's writings as well as author of the book *C. S. Lewis: A Companion & Guide*. He is also an adviser to the estate of C. S. Lewis.

Walter Hooper has been a source of recent controversy among some writers and Lewis scholars including Kathryn Lindskoog in her recent book *Sleuthing C. S. Lewis: More Light in the Shadowlands*. However, Hooper's claims to have known Lewis and to have served as his temporary secretary (during the absence of Lewis's brother, Warnie) in 1963 have been substantiated by others who knew Lewis, including Douglas Gresham. And there is no doubt that Mr. Hooper has focused much of his career as a writer and editor on the life and work of C. S. Lewis. His contributions to this book as an interview subject are substantial.

Dabney Hart, Ph.D.—English professor, Lewis scholar, and lecturer. As a student, Dabney Hart met C. S. Lewis during his time at Cambridge University as part of her graduate studies on his work. "He had a good handshake," Hart recalled, "and a lovely, warm, welcoming smile. He wasn't striking or distinctive-looking in any way, just pleasant." Hart went on to author numerous articles on Lewis as well as the book *Through the Open Door: A New Look at C. S. Lewis* for the University of Alabama Press. Today, Hart is an associate professor of English at Georgia State University in Atlanta.

Lyle Dorsett, Ph.D.—professor, author, lecturer. A professor of evangelism and spiritual formation at Illinois's Wheaton College and Graduate School, Dorsett is the author of numerous articles and books on C. S. Lewis, including *And God Came In: A Biography of Joy Davidman.* Dorsett is also the editor of *The Essential C. S. Lewis* and coeditor (with Marjorie Mead) of *C. S. Lewis: Letters to Children.* He is currently writing a spiritual biography on Lewis. Dorsett is the former director of the Marion E. Wade Center at Wheaton College and is a senior pastor at the Church of the Great Shepherd in Wheaton.

Christopher W. Mitchell, Ph.D.—pastor, missionary, director of the Marion E. Wade Center at Wheaton College. After receiving his doctorate from the University of St. Andrews (Scotland), where his concentration was historical theology, Mitchell spent several years as a Christian missionary, including time in both India and Haiti. As director of the Wade Center, Mitchell has lectured widely on C. S. Lewis and published articles including "Bearing the Weight of Glory: The Cost of C. S. Lewis's Witness" and "University Battles: C. S. Lewis and the Oxford Socratic Club," along with numerous contributions to journals and other publications. He is currently working on a book-length study of C. S. Lewis and the Oxford Socratic Club. Mitchell is also an assistant professor of theological studies at Wheaton College and book-review editor of *Seven: An Anglo-American Literary Review.*

Colin Manlove— professor, writer, Lewis scholar. Born in Falkirk, Scotland, in 1942, Manlove received a M.A. degree in English language and literature at Edinburgh University. He then went on to take a B. Litt. postgraduate degree at Pembroke College, Oxford, with a thesis on English fantasy. He became a lecturer at Edinburgh University in 1967 and was made Doctor of Letters in 1990. In 1993, Manlove retired from the university and has continued writing.

Manlove has authored numerous books on fantasy, science fiction, Shakespeare, and English literature from 1600–1800. His extensive writings on C. S. Lewis include *C. S. Lewis: His Literary Achievement* (1987) and *The Chronicles of Narnia: The Patterning of a Fantastic World* (1993). He has also written approximately forty articles and essays. It is Manlove's belief that fantasy can best be described in terms of its country of origin, and he has plans for a book on the fantasy of different European countries.

Manlove was first drawn to C. S. Lewis after reading *The Problem of Pain*, which excited him intellectually. He later read *Perelandra*, which, he says, "has never failed to awaken wonder." Years of teaching Lewis texts to students "continually highlighted new aspects of his work, which, like any good literature, revealed fresh perspectives with each reading," said Manlove. "Lewis's mind and work have brought light to my life, and I look forward one day to saying so face to face."

The common denominators among those included in this oral history on C. S. Lewis are their passion for Lewis's work and their commitment to sharing personal insights into C. S. Lewis the man, the writer, the teacher, and the creator of magical worlds.

We are grateful for the time they shared with us, for their participation in the interview process, and for their commitment to our efforts to share the story of C. S. Lewis on television and in various forms of educational media and print.

The central story of my life is about nothing else . . . I call it Joy. . . . It might equally well be called a particular kind of unhappiness or grief. But then it is the kind that we want. . . . All Joy reminds. It is never a possession, always a desire for something longer ago or further away or still about to be.

—C. S. Lewis

Surprised by Joy

CHAPTER ONE

ORIGINS

On November 22, 1963, American president John F. Kennedy was killed by a sniper's bullet in Dallas, Texas. Thousands of miles to the east, the Beatles released their second album in London, a soon-to-be classic called *With the Beatles*. Acclaimed British writer Aldous Huxley died at the age of sixty-nine. And in the cloistered, academic world of Oxford, England, the long career of C. S. Lewis ended with his death. He was sixty-four years old.

C. S. Lewis's career was defined by scholarly pursuits in medieval literature, apologetics writings, and an imagination that brought magic into the lives of children and adults through a book series called The Chronicles of Narnia. His classic satire, *The*

Screwtape Letters, had made Lewis a household name in both England and the United States. And books such as *The Problem of Pain, Miracles, A Grief Observed,* and *Mere Christianity* had solidified Lewis's reputation among the greatest Christian writers in the English language.

Still, at the time of his death, few people realized the scope and significance of his work and little was known about his life. It's only now, with the distance imposed by time and the insights of a new generation of scholars, that we're beginning to realize his powerful contributions to literature and to learning.

According to Dabney Hart, "C. S. Lewis was an Oxford scholar. First and foremost, he was a great teacher."

"First and foremost, he was a Christian," countered Douglas Gresham. "Secondly he was a scholar."

"He was a fellow at Magdalen College, Oxford," said Lyle Dorsett. "He was an Oxford graduate himself. He had two degrees from Oxford. He spent his life in the academic world doing lectures and holding tutorials. He was also a Christian and that marks who he is and the world-view he brings to his subject."

"Lewis was very interested in the universal whole," said Colin Manlove. "He had a science-fictional interest in 'the wider,' as in outside this world. He had a fascination with strange images. He was particularly good at evoking wonder.

"He said, 'You can make anything by writing. You can make a world of your own. You can do what you want with it as long as it holds together.' He also said, 'I'm a dinosaur. I don't belong. I come from a past age.' Lewis had many Edwardian values."

According to Chris Mitchell, "Lewis was a great writer, literary critic, literary historian, writer of children's fantasy literature.

"He made the statement that the things he asserted most rigorously and vigorously are things he resisted long and accepted late," continued Mitchell. "And he basically brought all of his understanding, his argumentative skills, his vast learning to bear under defense of the Christian faith."

"He prayed a great deal," said Walter Hooper. "I don't think I've ever come across a person who prayed so much—in a train, on a bus, on a walk, or just standing outside. The thing that struck me about him more than anything was that this man really loved God."

"He dealt with topics that span races and genders and generations," said Dorsett. "'Who are we?' 'Where are we going?' 'Is there a God?' These are questions that we all have. Thoughtful people wrestle with these things. And Lewis was very good at helping us understand them without being overly preachy."

"He became what most people would say is the leading Christian apologist of the second half of the twentieth century," said Hart. "And other people would say he became the author of the most important children's series of the twentieth century. So you can't answer that with just one simple answer. He was a complex man."

———◆———

A complex man. Clive Staples Lewis, who published under the name C. S. Lewis and whom friends called Jack, was born in Belfast, in Northern Ireland, on November 29, 1898. The second of two sons,

LEWIS AT AGE ONE, 1899.

he lived in a boyhood home called Little Lea with his father, Albert James Lewis, his mother, Flora Augusta Hamilton Lewis, and his brother, Warren. In all that's been written about Lewis's childhood, two things stand out: the quality of his imagination and the deep sense of loss he felt at the early death of his mother.

Lewis's imagination was visible in the games he and his brother, Warnie, would play in the attic at Little Lea, such as creating a fictional world they called "Boxen." Because his parents thought he had a weak chest (many diseases, such as typhoid and scarlet fever, were prevalent in Belfast at the time), they often kept Lewis inside, especially on the frequent rainy days. Lewis and Warnie were, at this early age, best friends. They learned to draw and Lewis began creating stories. By age ten, Lewis had begun writing.

It was also during his life at Little Lea that Lewis developed his lifelong passion for reading. In his autobiographical book, *Surprised by Joy*, Lewis wrote:

I am the product of long corridors, empty sunlit rooms, upstairs indoor silences, attics explored in solitude, distant noises of gurgling cisterns and pipes, and the noise of wind under the tiles. Also, of

C. S. "JACK" LEWIS AND HIS BROTHER, WARREN, BICYCLING IN NORTHERN IRELAND, 1908.

endless books. My father bought all the books he read and never got rid of any of them. There were books in the study, books in the drawing room, books in the cloakroom, books (two deep) in the great bookcase on the landing, books in a bedroom, books piled as high as my shoulder in the cistern attic, books of all kinds reflecting every transient stage of my parents' interest, books readable and unreadable, books suitable for a child and books most emphatically not. Nothing was forbidden me. In seeming endless rainy afternoons I took volume

LEWIS'S MOTHER, FLORENCE AUGUSTA HAMILTON.

after volume from the shelves. I had always the same certainty of finding a book that was new to me as a man who walks into a field has of finding a new blade of grass.[1]

The second thing that stood out about Lewis's childhood was the deep sadness and resentment he experienced at the loss of his mother. Flora Lewis died of abdominal cancer when Lewis was just nine years old.

"Clearly, the death of Lewis's mother was a watershed in his life," commented Mitchell. "And it was doubly difficult because with the loss of his mother, he and his father began to grow apart. His father didn't recover. Now I don't think it was as bleak as some people would make it out to be, especially if you read the letters that are exchanged in the family papers. There's a real affection by his father, but his father was never able to really engage in the way that I think the boys really wanted him to after that. It isn't because he wasn't willing. I think he was just incapable. But the best person to talk about it would have been Lewis, and he really didn't say a whole lot about it."

It was during the grief that surrounded the loss of his mother that Lewis began to question the existence of God. According to Gresham, "The great tragedy of his childhood was the loss of his mother when he was a little boy. That changed the whole pattern of his life. As the son of two devoted Christians, Jack went to church and believed in God and in Jesus Christ. But his mother's death, I think, was the first wedge that was driven into that masonry."

LITTLE LEA, LEWIS'S CHILDHOOD HOME IN BELFAST.

As an early adolescent, Lewis began to drift toward atheism. Dorsett said, "When his mother was dying of cancer, he prayed and asked God to heal her, and, of course, she died. And he believed at that time that God either wasn't there or if he was there, he was just cruel. And he saw God as either impotent to do anything about it or very cruel in the way he worked with things. And so, the problem of pain and the problem of evil came into his life at an early age."

Lewis himself reflected on the tragedy in *Surprised by Joy*: "*With my mother's death all settled happiness, all that was tranquil, reliable, disappeared from my life. There was to be much fun, many pleasures, great stabs of Joy; but no more of the old security. It was sea and islands now; the great continent had sunk like Atlantis.*"[2]

"Lewis's subsequent upbringing by people other than his parents and the influences of other people began to shatter the structure of his Christian faith," said Gresham. "Eventually, at one of his schools, he lost it completely. Being a young man with an immensely powerful intellect and rational mind, he soon began to try to rationalize everything around him, and to rationalize God out of his life. One of his tutors, William T. Kirkpatrick, was a rationalist and a humanist. He had the influence on Jack of making him think and search for truth much more deeply than he had before."

Shortly after Flora's death, Albert Lewis sent his son to join his brother, Warnie, at Wynyard School in Watford, England. A

ARTHUR RACKHAM ILLUSTRATION FROM
WAGNER'S *Siegfried and the Twilight of the Gods.*

brutal headmaster made the experience nearly insufferable for both boys. However, Lewis had a dramatic literary experience at another boarding school in 1911. There Lewis discovered Richard Wagner's *Siegfried and the Twilight of the Gods,* a story of Norse mythology. The idea of "northernness" was firmly planted in his imagination. Given his interest in fictional worlds (he'd read Milton's *Paradise Lost* by age ten), Lewis grew to love these mystical stories of magic, dragons, and dwarfs. It was at this time that Lewis really discovered literature on the legends and mythology of northern Europe.

"For him, I think literature was the primary source of his imagination," said

Hart. "His imagination was just saturated with the myths of the north, which he referred to and used very seldom, I think, because he knew that most of his readers would not be famil-iar with those as they would be with the Arthurian legends or with the myths of the Greeks and Romans. But he loved Norse mythology."

By 1913, Lewis was gaining attention for his classical studies at England's Malvern College. While there, he authored *Loki Bound*, a pessimistic tragedy about Norse gods. It was a turbulent period in his life and he was clearly searching. As he recalled in *Surprised by Joy*, it was during this time that he became an atheist. Lewis wrote: *"I was at this time living, like so many Atheists . . . in a whirl of contradictions. I maintained that God did not exist. I was also very angry with God for not existing. I was equally angry with Him for cre-ating a world."*[3]

While in Belfast in 1914 a short time later, Lewis befriended a boy named Arthur Greeves. They remained lifelong friends, exchanging letters until Lewis's death. It was in a letter to Greeves in October 1916 that Lewis wrote, *"I believe in no religion. There is absolutely no proof for any of them, and from a philosophical standpoint Christianity is not even the best. All religions, that is, all mythologies, to give them their proper name, are merely man's own invention, Christ as much as Loki."*[4]

As he had been at Wynyard School, Lewis became discouraged with Malvern College, and, with the reluctant support of his father, he left to pursue his studies elsewhere. From 1914 to 1916, his intellectual challenges grew under the tutelage of William T. Kirkpatrick. For approximately two and a half years, Lewis lived

> "Lewis was very interested in the universal whole. He had science-fictional interest in 'the wider,' as in outside this world. He had a fascination with strange images. He was particularly good at evoking wonder."
>
> — COLIN MANLOVE

with Kirkpatrick in the village of Great Bookham in Surrey. He described his time in Great Bookham as among the happier times in his life—a sharp contrast to his earlier studies at Wynyard and Malvern.

W. T. Kirkpatrick had been Albert Lewis's headmaster when he'd attended Lurgan College years earlier, and they'd maintained a relationship over the years. Kirkpatrick had a reputation as a rationalist and a logician, and Lewis learned quickly to use his intellect in all kinds of academic discussion. A student of languages, Lewis also immersed himself in Greek, Latin, French, Italian, and German. Far more than his previous school experiences, Lewis's studying with Kirkpatrick prepared him well for the academic life he would soon undertake at Oxford.

"During his time with William T. Kirkpatrick, Lewis became a confirmed atheist in his thinking and viewed Christianity from that point on as myth," said Mitchell. "He loved myth, but myth was not fact. Myth was something that was false. And that's the same category in which he put Christianity. He just lumped Christianity in with all the other myths that basically distracted people from truth and reality and facts."

Lewis spent much of his time at Great Bookham reading northern mythology and learning to write poetry. It was also during this time that he first read George Macdonald's *Phantastes,* the book that introduced the idea of holiness into his life. According to Lewis, *"I had already been waist deep in Romanticism; and likely enough, at any moment, to flounder into its darker and more evil forms, slithering down the steep descent that leads from the love of strangeness to that of eccentricity and thence to that of perversity.* Now Phantastes *. . . had about it a sort of cool, morning innocence. . . . What it actually did to me was to convert, even to baptize . . . my imagination."*[5]

In December 1916 Lewis made his first visit to Oxford for a classical scholarship at University College. In a letter to his father, Lewis said: *"This place has surpassed my wildest dreams; I never saw anything so beautiful."*[6]

"There's just something about Oxford," said Mitchell, "something about the buildings and the spires and the closed doors that are sometimes just a little ways open, and you peek in and there's this garden and grass and then all these little windows."

To the uninitiated visitor, the cloistered colleges that comprise Oxford University present an otherworldly quality. Ornate, often medieval-styled buildings are adorned with gargoyles and spires, and the cobblestone walks and vast green courtyards

OXFORD'S HIGH STREET.

trimmed to perfection create a campus setting. Because the colleges are walled off to the general public, there's a mysterious quality about them, leading a visitor to wonder what great minds reside within . . . and what great achievements are yet to come. Like many first-time visitors, Lewis was equally inspired by the long tradition of great thinkers, scholars, and writers whose work lent the university a perceived sense of inspiration and immortality.

"Lewis loved Oxford," continued Mitchell. "He loved the spires, he loved the life in Oxford. And part of it was that he loved the life of the mind. And Oxford is a wonderful place for those who love the life of the mind."

"It's known as 'the city of dreaming spires' for very good rea-

"He prayed a great deal. I don't think
I've ever come across a person who prayed so
much—in a train, on a bus, on a walk, or just
standing outside. The thing that struck me
about him more than anything was that
this man really loved God."

—WALTER HOOPER

son," said Gresham. "But initially it's the college architecture, and the spires that reach up out of the mists of the river valley that impact you. It has a sort of quiet, sedentary atmosphere about it, once you get over the roar of traffic and so on. It has been, for hundreds and hundreds of years, a center for learning as opposed to training. It was, at least in Jack's day, a community of deep thinking intellectual men and women. It had an atmosphere of learning, and there was a strong sense of the search for truth and knowledge in all sorts of areas."

According to Mitchell, "Lewis was, in his conception of reality, an idealist. That is, behind reality is mind, and for him that would be God's mind. And therefore, he took ideas seriously in ways many people don't. Oxford took ideas seriously and he loved that."

The people of Oxford also contributed to his excitement about

Top: Three generations of Lewises, about 1900. C. S. is the baby at far right.
Bottom: Lewis with family and servants at Little Lea, 1905.

being there. Mitchell added, "So many of the great ideas of the western English world have come out of that center—people that he had read and loved—and to think that now he's there himself! He knew Oxford through the reading of so many people who lived and generated thoughts in that area. When Lewis first came to Oxford, it was a great day in his life because of what Oxford stood for."

From the time he was accepted into Oxford University in 1917 until his death forty-six years later, Lewis made Oxford his home. From those auspicious grounds, C. S. Lewis launched many great journeys of both mind and spirit.

CHAPTER TWO

FRIENDSHIP

$\mathcal{A}$s he began his student life at Oxford on April 28, 1917, Lewis's faith in the existence of God was further challenged. England was deeply embroiled in World War I when Lewis, then a subject of Ireland, enlisted in the British Armed Services just five months after his college enrollment.

"What happens to a man when he goes into combat?" asked Lyle Dorsett. "What happens to him when his best friend is killed in combat? When men around him, men under his command are killed?"

Commissioned as a second lieutenant in the Third Battalion of the Somerset Light Infantry, Lewis arrived on the front lines in France on his nineteenth birthday in November 1917—just twelve days after arriving in the country. The following January, Lewis was hospitalized for nearly a month in the British Red Cross Hospital in Le Tréport while suffering from trench fever. During his recovery, a letter he wrote reflected a lighthearted view of his atheism: *"The gods hate me—and naturally enough considering my usual attitude towards them."*[1]

While serving on the front, Lewis distinguished himself by help-ing in the capture of nearly sixty German soldiers. His service ended when he was wounded by friendly fire during the Battle of Arras near Lilliers. A shell burst, leaving shrapnel lodged in Lewis's chest and hands. After recuperating in military hospitals in London, Lewis eventually returned to his studies at Oxford in 1919.

According to Dorsett, "World War I had a profound impact on him. But in his era, being an Englishman and living in the early twentieth century, the last thing you did was pour it all out. I can't believe that there's a man that has been in combat and sur-vived who doesn't say, 'Why did I survive?' and 'Somehow I've got to earn it, what am I going to do? What do I do with this?' It made Lewis wrestle with why he lives and so many of his com-rades die. 'Why? What's going on here? Is there a purpose? Is this just random?'"

Among the wartime casualties, Lewis lost a very good friend, Irishman E. F. C. "Paddy" Moore. The same age, they'd shared a room together at the Officer Training Corps at Oxford's Keble College before going to the front. The effect on Lewis of both the training and the war was significant for many reasons. According

JACK LEWIS AND "PADDY" MOORE, OXFORD, 1917.

to Dorsett, Lewis's experience on the front lines "was like a driving engine in him." Dorsett believes it contributed to Lewis's later writing on the problem of pain and the problem of evil "because he sees it in the death of his mother, in the death of his best friend, and on down the line."

During the time of their military training, Lewis had also become close to Paddy's mother, forty-five-year-old Jane King Moore, and Paddy's younger sister, eleven-year-old Maureen. Mrs. Moore had separated from her husband, and, knowing that casualties on the western front were high, she'd moved to Oxford with her daughter to be closer to Paddy before he departed to France. Shortly before leaving for the front, Lewis and Paddy Moore made a pact.

LEWIS WITH JANE KING MOORE AND HER DAUGHTER, MAUREEN.

"Paddy and Jack had agreed that if either of them died and the other survived, the survivor would take care of the other's family," said Dorsett. "So when Paddy died, Jack was good to his word and he took care of Mrs. Moore and her daughter, Maureen."

During Lewis's convalescence, he paid regular visits to Mrs.

Moore. She'd suffered greatly at the loss of her son and many suggest that Lewis, who'd become somewhat estranged from his father, was in need of her company and her motherly kindness. Whatever the circumstances that drew them together, a close bond was the result. And, as soon as he was well enough, Lewis intended to honor the promise he'd made to his friend.

Following two terms of required residence at University College, Lewis rented accommodations for himself, Mrs. Moore, and Maureen in Headington, at the time a small community roughly four miles east of the university. The relationship that unfolded between Lewis and Mrs. Moore remains in question with varying opinions from scholars and historians. Was it a sexual relationship? Or was she more like a surrogate mother to Lewis, providing a sense of family life he'd missed out on since the death of his own mother eleven years earlier?

"I interviewed Maureen," said Dorsett. "She said she suspected that there was something going on in the early years. He was about half her age, but stranger things have happened. And they had a strange relationship. A man who knew both of them very well is confident that they did have an affair early on, and that this is part of why Jack has some problems with how he will deal with her and what he will do. It was one of those situations in which there were regrets, but they went forward."

"Lewis clearly enjoyed her company very much," said Hooper. "If you read his diary, that's evident." At least in the beginning, Lewis considered Mrs. Moore a close companion. In fact, while serving in France, Lewis wrote and thanked his friend Arthur

"The last thing [Lewis] would have
liked was a lot of sherry parties with a lot
of chitchat and small talk. I'm amazed at how
many letters I've found over the years where
somebody writes and invites him to do
something, and he'd say, 'Oh, I'd love to, but
I can't get away. I have sort of this surrogate
mother, Mrs. Moore, that I have to take care
of. I wish I could come but. . . .' I think if
he didn't have Mrs. Moore he would have
had to find her or invent her, because
she was his excuse for avoiding a lot of
socially unpleasant things."

—LYLE DORSETT

Greeves for corresponding with Mrs. Moore during his absence.
He wrote that he was glad *the two people who mean most to me in
the world are in touch.*[2] Lewis also wrote to his father at different
times of his affection for Mrs. Moore. Regardless of whether it

was a love affair or a surrogate mother-son relationship, it was an association of which Albert Lewis did not approve.

According to Mitchell, "Some say that early on it was an infatuation and there was a sexual encounter and then later, especially after Lewis became a Christian, that was cut off. The relationship changed."

"If it did happen, it didn't last for very long," said Hooper. "I think Lewis's conversion to Christianity would have certainly put an end to that. But Lewis had things that he was ashamed of, like the treatment of his father. I think that was the biggest thing for him in later years to deal with, the fact that he had been so unkind to his father. I do know he went to confession weekly once he started. And he was a man who really did look at himself very hard and if he had a sin, he would spot it. And I would imagine the things about Mrs. Moore and the things about his father both loomed large in his confessions. We'll never know what went on, and we shouldn't even try to find out. But I can't admire him enough for living up to his promise and seeing it through to the end."

"I think that Mrs. Moore, whose marriage had failed and who then lost her son in the war, really was looking for and needed a substitute for those people, and she found a good one in Jack," said Gresham.

It was, in many ways, a healing relationship for both people at a challenging time in their lives. According to Gresham, Lewis even referred to Mrs. Moore at times as his mother.

Without question, life with Mrs. Moore and her daughter,

Maureen, held challenge for Lewis. He was forced to juggle the life of a young academic with that of a care provider. He wrote:

> During this time it was unfortunate that my first spring flood of Dymer [a book-length narrative poem Lewis began in 1922 and published in 1926] should coincide with a burst of marmalade-making and spring-cleaning on Mrs. Moore's part, which led without intermission into packing. I managed to get through a good deal of writing in the intervals of jobbing in the kitchen and doing messages. . . . I also kept my temper nearly all the time. Domestic drudgery is excellent as an alternative to idleness or to hateful thoughts—which is perhaps poor Mrs. Moore's reason for piling it on all the time; as an alternative to the work one is longing to do and able to do . . . it is maddening. No one's fault; the curse of Adam.[3]

Yet it was during the early part of his relationship with Mrs. Moore that his career as a prolific writer began. In 1919, Lewis, using the pen name Clive Hamilton, published his first book, a small volume of lyric poetry called *Spirits in Bondage*. In many ways, his first published work began to define his spiritual search. In a letter to his father, Lewis wrote: *"This little success gives me a pleasure which is perhaps childish, and yet akin to greater things."* When describing the theme Lewis said: *"Nature is wholly diabolical and malevolent and that God, if he exists, is outside and in opposition to the cosmic arrangement."*[4]

Throughout his time caring for the Moores, Lewis often spoke highly of Mrs. Moore's influence in his life. Yet based on the opinions and writings of Lewis's brother, Warnie, there's ongoing debate about the impact the caretaker responsibilities had on Lewis's work. "I think it was a dreadful burden," said Hooper. "But the man who wrote *The Four Loves* was not a man to dump somebody out of the house."

> "It was inevitable that Tolkien and Lewis meet. . . . It was not inevitable that they become friends—but they did."
>
> —WALTER HOOPER

According to Manlove, "Lewis was imposed on by Mrs. Moore, who was constantly calling him away from what he was doing. He hardly had a half-hour at a time to write before he would be doing something like washing up or sweeping the floor."

"The burdens of his relationship with Mrs. Moore were manifold," concurred Gresham. "First of all, she was an eccentric lady. She needed constant reassurance of his devotion. And so she would allow him to write for about ten or fifteen minutes, then call him away to some trivial job in the kitchen or whatever, constantly, all day long.

"But while these things were burdensome, they also resulted

in some of the finest writing the world has ever seen. Some of Jack's finest work was a result of that period of time. The constant interruptions may have allowed him to train his mind to be far more acute in concentration on what he was writing when he was writing it."

Gresham further insisted that Mrs. Moore was not a purely selfish individual. "It's easy enough to paint Mrs. Moore as an ogre," said Gresham, "but there was a great deal of good in her. She was an intensely charitable person."

There's also an argument to be made that Lewis enjoyed a good deal of security from the relationship as well, security that went beyond the emotional needs of his earlier years. Lewis was not known to enjoy certain social gatherings and preferred, when possible, to be at home writing.

According to Dorsett, "The last thing he would have liked was a lot of sherry parties with a lot of chitchat and small talk. I'm amazed at how many letters I've found over the years where somebody writes and invites him to do something, and he'd say, 'Oh, I'd love to, but I can't get away. I have sort of this surrogate mother, Mrs. Moore, that I have to take care of. I wish I could come but. . . .' I think if he didn't have Mrs. Moore he would have had to find her or invent her, because she was his excuse for avoiding a lot of socially unpleasant things."

Mitchell believes, "There was an evolution in Lewis's relationship with Mrs. Moore. And toward the end, she was probably not easy to get on with. Lewis probably did suffer under that, but to his credit, he didn't complain, even while his colleagues often

ALBERT LEWIS WITH SONS WARREN AND JACK.

wondered why he did it. Owen Barfield [a Lewis friend and member of the Inklings] called it a 'genius of the will'—that when Lewis decided something, he followed through with it. He was a loyal friend."

During the early part of Lewis's relationship with the Moores, he and his father had a difficult relationship at best. Albert Lewis had always had trouble dealing with his own grief at the loss of his wife and he never approved of the close relationship between his son and Mrs. Moore. According to George Sayer's biography on Lewis called *Jack*, the relationship caused a great deal of worry for Albert and further widened the rift between father and son. Still, Lewis remained loyal to his commitment to Paddy

Jack, Warren, Albert, and neighbor.

Jack, Albert, and Warren on an outing with the family, 1911.

Moore. He looked after Mrs. Moore for thirty-two years, until her death in 1951.

A loyal friend. Nothing characterized Lewis more than his commitment to friendship. And he found it in abundance at Oxford.

"One of the finest things that happened to Jack in his early years at Oxford was that he gathered around himself a group of friends who were among the very finest minds in the world at the time," said Gresham. "And they were friends for life. This friendship that developed was a huge part of shaping his whole being. And they called themselves the Inklings."

"Lewis was a social being but only within clearly defined parameters," said Mitchell. It was "common interest with these Inklings. They came together and they loved the same things he loved. They loved good literature, loved to argue, loved fun."

"He liked friendship and conversation—especially good conversation over a pint of beer in a pub," said Hooper. "He loved the atmosphere of pubs. One of the greatest moments for him, always, was the meeting of the Inklings on Tuesday morning. And over a cup or pint of beer, they shared an hour of conversation about things they all loved."

According to Hooper, it's hard to say exactly when the Inklings began their meetings. But by the early 1930s, the weekly rendezvous had become part of Lewis's routine. Lewis had been elected to a fellowship in English language and literature at

BUILDING WHERE LEWIS LIVED DURING HIS YEARS AT MAGDALEN COLLEGE.

Magdalen College, Oxford, in May 1925. Considered one of the most beautiful of the roughly thirty colleges that make up the university, Magdalen was a place where Lewis maintained a room and study throughout his tenure there. His rooms overlooked the famous deer park and Addison's Walk, a trail that runs alongside the Cherwell River. When Lewis wasn't writing, reading, tutoring students, or caring for Mrs. Moore at their home in Headington, he usually stayed at Magdalen overnight and frequently entertained friends such as J. R. R. Tolkien and Hugo Dyson.

Others, including some from outside the university, soon joined the Inklings as well. "Warnie was one of the first to join," said Hooper. "Though he didn't write many papers, he liked to listen. He loved good conversation. Then along came Neville Coghill, the great translator of Chaucer, Lord David Cecil, the biographer and professor, then others." The group also included Lewis's lawyer, Owen Barfield, and A. C. Harwood, a schoolmaster. Meetings of the Inklings took place weekly at the Eagle and Child pub on Tuesday mornings and on regular evenings in Lewis's college rooms.

Gresham explained, "It became a loose collection of some of

the greatest writers of the century. They were men who, first and foremost, shared interests in literature, and they would get together to talk about not only literature and language but also about the works that they themselves were writing. It was a normal practice in one of these informal meetings for whoever was working on something at the time to read passages of it aloud to the rest of the group and to invite criticism. And I think that the process of honing their words with great minds of equal interest in literature is one of the things that characterizes the finished works of these men on such a high level."

PUB WHERE THE INKLINGS MET.

"Few people in Oxford or anywhere else would have been qualified to read one of Lewis's books and say, 'Hey, this is not working,' or 'You've got to rewrite that,'" said Hooper. "But that's what these men were expected to do. If someone had a paper to read, they would read it. For instance, Lewis read the whole of *The Problem of Pain*, chapter by chapter, to that group. He read the whole of *The Screwtape Letters* to them. And it was there in the Inklings meetings that Tolkien read *The Lord of the Rings*. Imagine the richness of those readings. And if they didn't like something, they went at it hammer and tongs. So I'm sure Lewis was greatly influenced by them and what they said. They were a wonderful sounding board."

Gresham added, "I think it was the men who joined the Inklings, the conversations, the flow of ideas, the repartee, and the continual dialectic that went on—those were the building blocks of Jack's intellect."

"What he mainly enjoyed was not just the free criticism, but the friendship," said Hooper. "As Lewis said in *The Four Loves* in the chapter on friendship, 'When two people suddenly discover that they like not only the same things but see the same truth, in that moment a friendship is born.' That's what it's about."

While all of the Inklings were important to Lewis, the friendship with J. R. R. Tolkien was special for many reasons. "It was inevitable," said Hooper, "that Tolkien and Lewis meet. When Lewis became a member of the English faculty in 1925, Tolkien had arrived at almost the same time to teach Anglo-Saxon. And in 1926, at a meeting of the faculty, Lewis and Tolkien met. It was not inevitable that they become friends—but they did."

"In terms of sheer encouragement of one another, they each found someone who liked the same things as the other person," said Mitchell. "The story is told that at a point they sort of agreed that nobody was writing the types of books that they liked to read, so they decided that they would do it. And that kind of camaraderie has benefits that you really can't articulate. I think most of the chemistry between them falls in that realm."

Many of the powerful friendships Lewis forged in his early years at Oxford stayed with him throughout his adult life. In particular, the relationship between Lewis and Tolkien stands out. There are few times in history where two talents of such great stature have been united by friendship and professional camaraderie. For more than thirty years, they shared a passion for myth, fantasy, and magical worlds. Eventually, a shared faith would also play a role in the work they left behind for future generations.

CHAPTER THREE

THE TRUE MYTH

The joy and companionship Lewis received from his friendships did not soothe the pain he felt over his strained relationship with his father. During the summer of 1929, Albert Lewis was diagnosed with cancer. Warnie Lewis was serving the military in China, so Jack returned to Ireland and became, for a time, his father's caregiver. It was a period of great emotional upheaval for Lewis. While in Belfast, Lewis wrote in a letter to Owen Barfield: *"Every room is soaked with the bogeys of childhood—the awful 'rows' with my father, the awful returnings to school, and also with the old pleasures of an unusually ignoble adolescence."*[1]

On September 22 Lewis returned to Oxford to prepare for the

fall term. Three days later, his father died. Because the two men had been somewhat estranged for many years, Albert Lewis's death forced Jack into a period of reflection and self-examination. It's also been speculated that his father's death helped further his journey toward Christianity.

Once again, literature proved a dramatic influence. "When he read G. K. Chesterton's *Everlasting Man,* he began to see that maybe Christianity was not so intellectually 'in the dark' as he had thought," said Mitchell. "And so there's this journey. And at this point he was really looking for reasons not to believe in the Christian faith, and yet without him even trying, things are coming into his life to force him to look at it and say, 'Well, maybe it's not such an open-and-shut case.'"

Lewis himself admitted, *"In reading Chesterton, as in reading MacDonald, I did not know what I was letting myself in for. A young man who wishes to remain a sound Atheist cannot be too careful in his reading. There are traps everywhere—'Bibles laid open, millions of surprises . . . fine nets and stratagems.' God is, if I may say it, very unscrupulous."*[2]

"He was the most reluctant believer in the United Kingdom," noted Dorsett. "But he couldn't help himself. He was drawn to God. God kept drawing him to him. He also discovered that some of the authors he loved most were Christians. Milton, for example, or Spenser."

Though it may not have been common among scholars during Lewis's time in Oxford, many of his friends and members of the Inklings were Christians, including Tolkien, Barfield,

"In reading Chesterton, as in
reading MacDonald, I did not know what
I was letting myself in for. A young man
who wishes to remain a sound Atheist
cannot be too careful in his reading.
There are traps everywhere—'Bibles
laid open, millions of surprises . . . fine
nets and stratagems.' God is, if I may
say it, very unscrupulous."

—C. S. LEWIS
Surprised by Joy

Dyson, and Coghill. They happened to be among the people
whom he found most interesting. "And what did he do with
that?" asked Dorsett. "Well, he couldn't totally discount it.
Concomitant with that was this longing in his soul." Lewis
yearned for love and a sense of home, though he'd yet to find
either. "His mother died. His father let him down," continued
Dorsett. "He had these longings that he couldn't explain and he
didn't know what to do with them. At the same time, he was a
very thoughtful man, and he had to deal with some hard questions and issues."

In the search for answers, Lewis was forced to question ideas he'd held on to for several years, including his own "chronological snobbery," said Mitchell. "Lewis described this as the idea that whatever is the common thought of the age is what is acceptable. That which is dated is then, on that account, discredited. Slowly, however, Lewis began to challenge his own thinking. 'If something is now passé, why?'" said Mitchell. "'Why did it go out of date and who argued against it and where? And was it a compelling argument?' In other words, the dismissal of past thought uncritically was no longer acceptable to Lewis; it was inadmissible. He began to realize he'd never really looked back, intellectually, at the arguments for Christianity. And he began to read people

ADDISON'S WALK, MAGDALEN COLLEGE.

who had. Like Chesterton. People who had a reason for their beliefs. The last thing that really came into play was what he would call the mythic elements of Christianity: redemption, a dying God, resurrection, God's sacrifice, blood—that sort of thing. Where had they all come from?"

Lewis's conversion to Christianity began to crystallize on a dreary September evening in 1931. Lewis had invited his friends J. R. R. Tolkien and Hugo Dyson to dine with him in his rooms at Magdalen College.

"It was raining outside and the wind was blowing," said

Hooper. "And after dinner they started talking about myth. This is something Lewis had thought about a great deal. But by 'myth' he meant something false, something that was not true."

The discussion was intense and after dinner, they decided to continue the debate while walking along Addison's Walk, a footpath that winds along the river near Lewis's rooms.

"Lewis was longing for reality in the depths of his soul, but his mind wouldn't let him make such leaps because he knew too many things," said Dorsett. "One of the things that kept him from being a Christian was that he found in ancient mythology examples of gods coming to earth and dying. And so he said, 'This Christian story is a myth. There are other ones similar to it and they're much older, so why should I believe this?'"

"He always loved myth," said Mitchell. "But myth was not fact. Myth was something false and that's the same category in which he put Christianity."

"But Tolkien pushed him," continued Dorsett. "He said, 'Jack, don't you understand that pagan people had a glimpse through their imaginations of the truth that was going to happen, and they tell stories about what they're longing for? And that it actually happened two thousand years ago? It's not just in somebody's mind. It's not just a story. It's a place in history. There was a man named Jesus, and plenty of literature that was non-Christian testified to this, and to much of what he was like. And so this is the myth that became real.'"

No doubt wet and tired, they returned to Lewis's rooms and continued the debate. "By the time the evening ended about four in the morning and Tolkien went home, Lewis had realized that he had made this huge mistake," said Hooper.

"What he began to realize is that myth is not false," said Mitchell. "Myth participates in truth. And all these different story lines, mythic story lines, each reflect the truth."

"Lewis had been lumping everything together, when, in fact, he saw with Tolkien's and Hugo Dyson's help that other myths weren't true. They pointed to something else—that is that finally, in history, in Israel, in a particular place called Bethlehem, a particular woman did give birth to somebody who was the Son of God. So Lewis could then say that 'myth became fact,' and that "I know now we're dealing with real things—the real Incarnation, Crucifixion, Resurrection.' On that night Lewis became a Christian. He was no longer believing in something that was up in the sky or perhaps a dream. He now believed in real things brought down to earth by God when God's Son became man."

"It's rather like Lewis's idea of *Sehnsucht*," said Manlove, "meaning that if the image strikes you far enough, you will feel the spiritual base that it has. So Lewis believed that the myth, if rightly followed, if rightly experienced, would have an affective power which would suggest its true divine base."

Hart added, "Lewis recognized that myth is the truth that has survived. And the reason it's survived is that it appeals to the human imagination. Indeed, the ancient myths of all cultures represent the human imagination's attempt to express an understanding of the relationship between human beings and divine power.

And of course that's the reason there's so many similarities in the myths of so many different cultures."

Tolkien's role was, according to Hooper, a key to Lewis's conversion. "Tolkien showed Lewis that not all myths are lies. In the Greek and Norse myths there is a Christlike figure who turns out not to be true—but it affects people. What Tolkien showed Lewis was that through the pagan myths, God was hinting, in divine form, at something that one day would turn out to be true. And then, in the fullness of time, when God was ready, suddenly everything which for centuries they'd been talking about in different cultures, became true and factual. God became an actual man, Jesus."

"Some people get concerned when they learn about how many myths there are from different cultures that feature a dying God who comes back to life," said Hart. "And some of these myths do have striking similarities. For example, Dionysus is the son of a princess who is impregnated by Zeus, the king of the gods. And he is destroyed by his own followers, but then is brought back to life. Lewis said it stands to reason there are all these stories in different cultures because the human imagination has always tried to establish a link between the human and the divine, the natural and the supernatural. And when God decided to send his Son into the world, he followed a mythic pattern that human imagination had already established, because that would make it so much more convincing to people. The human imagination already had an idea about this."

"What happens with Christianity is that Christianity is true myth," said Mitchell. "It holds on to everything that is true, and it actually becomes historical fact. And the fact is that this dying God that all of these other cultures have talked about actually happened in Christianity. You can date it."

In an essay in his book *God in the Dock*, Lewis himself wrote:

As myth transcends thought, Incarnation transcends myth. The heart of Christianity is a myth which is also a fact. The old myth of the Dying God, *without ceasing to be myth,* comes down from the heaven of legend and imagination to the earth of history. *It happens*—at a particular date, in a particular place, followed by definable historical consequences. We pass from a Balder or Osiris, dying nobody knows when or where, to a historical Person crucified (it is all in order) *under Pontius Pilate.* By becoming fact it does not cease to be myth: that is the miracle.[3]

Lewis went on to describe his own appreciation for the mythical aspects of his faith:

Those who do not know that this great myth became Fact when the Virgin conceived are, indeed, to be pitied. But Christians also need to be reminded . . . that what became Fact was a Myth, that it carries with it into the world of Fact all the properties of a myth. God is more than a god, not less; Christ is more than Balder, not less. We must not be ashamed of the mythical radiance resting on our theology.[4]

At the heart of Lewis's conversion is a concept he called *Sehnsucht*. It is the "joy" he refers to in his *Surprised by Joy*. In that sense, *Sehnsucht* is the "longing" described by Lyle Dorsett when he said that Lewis had a "longing in his soul." *Sehnsucht* is like an internal, spiritual hunger for an association with God, even for inclusion in the world of God in a way that makes one complete.

In the preface to his narrative poem, "Dymer," Lewis wrote: *"From at least the age of six, romantic longing—Sehnsucht—had played an unusually central part in my experience. Such longing is in itself the very reverse of wishful thinking: it is more like thoughtful wishing."⁵*

Years later, in *Surprised by Joy*, Lewis elaborated on the concept of joy:

> In a sense the central story of my life is about nothing else. . . . It is that of an unsatisfied desire which is itself more desirable than any other satisfaction. I call it Joy, which is here a technical term and must be sharply distinguished both from Happiness and from Pleasure. Joy (in my sense) has indeed one characteristic, and one only, in common with them; the fact that anyone who has experienced it will want it again. Apart from that and considered only in its quality, it might almost equally well be called a particular kind of unhappiness or grief. But then it is a kind we want. I doubt whether anyone who has tasted it would ever, if both were in his power, exchange it for all the pleasures in the world. But then Joy is never in our power and pleasure often is.⁶

"And then the oddest thing happened. It's as though God decided to pull the rug out from under him. [Lewis] and Warnie went to the zoo that day where they were meeting other friends, and there was Lewis in the sidecar. When he started out for the zoo, he didn't believe that Jesus was the Son of God. And yet somehow, by the time he arrived at the zoo, he did. It's one of those instances where you can think and think, you can write out all sorts of theological works, but sometimes God just short-circuits the whole thing. He gets right in there and he says, 'I am who I am.' And this is the way it happened to Lewis. He didn't make up his mind about who Christ was. He was just on his way to the zoo. But when he got there, he believed. And he said, 'It's rather like a man coming awake. You don't quite know when you wake up, you just find suddenly, hey, I'm in bed, lying awake.'"

—WALTER HOOPER

The concept was implied in many of Lewis's other writings as well, such as this excerpt from *The Lion, the Witch and the Wardrobe* in The Chonicles of Narnia series: *"At the name of Aslan each one of the children felt something jump in its inside. . . . Susan felt as if some delicious smell or some delightful strain of music had just floated by her. And Lucy got the feeling you have when you wake up in the morning and realise that it is the beginning of the holidays or the beginning of summer."*[7]

"You can say he was a great lecturer, a wonderful broadcaster, all these other things," said Manlove. "But the distinctive thing about Lewis was his particular argument about joy, *Sehnsucht*, or spiritual yearning. It raised in him such longings and desires that he was completely overcome by them. It became sort of a leitmotif of his life, a lodestone of his life."

"The whole concept of longing was central for Lewis," agreed Mitchell. "Joy, in this sense, is his term for this universal longing of the human spirit that everyone has, and that he recognized early in his life. It's the longing itself. It's not a sense of satisfaction. Rather, it's the idea that there's a longing and that there's an object attached to it, but you don't know what the object is. And it drives the human person—always searching, in one way or another. The whole quest of the human experience is this longing. In Lewis's atheistic period, there was no room for the longing. It made no sense in the materialist world but it wouldn't go away. But his move first to theism, a belief in a personal God, and eventually to Christianity, affirmed that sense of longing. It proved that indeed there is an object, a true object for this longing, that does ultimately bring that kind of satisfaction. And the joy is the surprise. It was the very thing he ran from. That longing led him to Christ, the person of Christ specifically, and to Christianity."

Perhaps the truest expression of Lewis's concept of Joy was in his 1941 address to students at the University Church in Oxford. Called "The Weight of Glory," the address included these words:

> The sense that in this universe we are treated as strangers, the longing to be acknowledged, to meet with some response, to bridge some chasm that yawns between us and reality, is part of our inconsolable secret. And surely, from this point of view, the promise of glory, in the sense described, becomes highly relevant to our deep desire. For glory meant good report with God, acceptance by God, response, acknowledgment, and welcome into the heart of things. The door on which we have been knocking all our lives will open at last.
>
> . . . Apparently, then, our lifelong nostalgia, our longing to be reunited with something in the universe from which we now feel cut off, to be on the inside of some door which we have always seen from the outside, is no more neurotic fancy, but the truest index of our real situation. And to be at last summoned inside would be both glory and honour beyond all merits and also the healing of that old ache.[8]

Manlove believes that Lewis, in his conversion to Christianity, hoped not just to see but also to feel a pattern of holiness in the

Christian mythology. "Lewis said of stories that they're trying to capture an elusive 'something.' What we're trying to capture in our net of successive events is something that isn't successive at all. It's a state, not a procedure; it's a thing, not a narrative. And that thing, the narrative tries to embody. And Lewis's whole object, he said, in writing stories, is to capture for a few moments that bird before it flies off to its own country or wherever it came from. I think, to that extent, in writing what we may call 'myths,' he is hoping to capture that sense that will come through the stories. And it comes through from wonder, from the excitement of the novelty of the images, and the potency of the images in a way that they work as holy images in terms of *Sehnsucht* or desire."

The internal, ever-present longing that Lewis references—the sense of joy—changed with his conversion from atheist to theist to Christian. It might be said that for the first time, he felt at home. Though the feeling of joy and yearning never left him, he knew, at least, for what he had been longing.

Lewis's conversion into a spiritual, and, eventually, a deeply religious person was a slow one. Through his twenties and early thirties it was, for him, a largely intellectual process. That changed in 1931.

"Lewis's conversion to Christianity was not a tidy affair," said Hooper. "Most of the time he spends talking about conversion in *Surprised by Joy* is really to theism. He believed that God existed, but he didn't believe that Christ was the Son of God until later. The one comes in 1929 and the other in 1931, and even it's a bit untidy. It happened when his brother, Warnie, took him on his motorbike and sidecar to the Whipsnade Zoo.

"Lewis had been thinking for years about how Jesus Christ fits into this whole thing. He said, 'I know that he's a good example, he's an extraordinary man, but that's not enough. This is not what Christianity is about. It's not about an extraordinary man who was filled with light and was just better than most people. There's got to be more to it than that.' And what the Scriptures say is that he's the Son of God.

"And then the oddest thing happened," continued Hooper. "It's as though God decided to pull the rug out from under him. He and Warnie went to the zoo that day where they were meeting other friends, and there was Lewis in the sidecar. When he started out for the zoo, he didn't believe that Jesus was the Son of God. And yet somehow, by the time he arrived at the zoo, he did. It's one of those instances where you can think and think, you can write out all sorts of theological works, but sometimes God just short-circuits the whole thing. He gets right in there and he says, 'I am who I am.' And this is the way it happened to Lewis. He didn't make up his mind about who Christ was. He was just on his way to the zoo. But when he got there, he believed. And he said, 'It's rather like a man coming awake. You don't quite know when you wake up, you just find suddenly, hey, I'm in bed, lying awake.'"

"Despite his immense talent with words on mundane matters," said Gresham, "even he found himself lost in trying to describe the process of being hit over the head by the Holy Spirit of God.

I don't think even Saint Paul could describe what really happened on the road to Damascus. And Jack couldn't describe what happened on the road to Whipsnade Zoo. He just suddenly came face to face with the Holy Spirit of God."

By the autumn of 1931, C. S. Lewis had become a Christian. Up to that time, he'd been a respected scholar, a respected teacher, a gifted student, a caretaker to Mrs. Moore, and a good friend to many Oxford colleagues. But his writings, while interesting, were not yet notable. That seemed to change with his transformation to Christianity.

"Up until 1931 when he was converted, he was a man with great technical skills," said Hooper. "He could write. He was highly literate. But he had nothing to say. Even his great poem that he spent years on, 'Dymer,' is technically brilliant. It has hundreds and hundreds of beautiful lines, but it's not about anything much.

"Poem after poem was sent to journals, but most were not published. He received refusal after refusal and he became impatient. He was a man who thought, *I am a writer, I want to be a poet.* But when suddenly all he cared about was God, when he lost all ambition and cared about something other than himself, that's when it was safe to give him something to say. And that's when C. S. Lewis began to write all of those wonderful books."

CHAPTER FOUR

THE PROBLEM OF PAIN

*I*n October 1930, C. S. Lewis used money from the sale of his family home in Belfast to purchase a home in Headington Quarry. Mrs. Moore also contributed financially to the purchase and the house was legally hers. Located in a secluded, wooded area roughly four miles east of Oxford's Magdalen College, it was known as the Kilns. The house took its name from old brick kilns that, at that time, still stood on the property.

"Warnie moved there in 1932," said Hooper, "and the brothers came together like adjoining panes on a window sill. They got on famously. And they were sort of inseparable from that time on."

Lewis and Warnie lived at the Kilns for the rest of their lives.

C. S. AND WARREN LEWIS.

But they were rarely alone. At various times, Mrs. Moore, Maureen, Lewis, Warnie, Fred Paxford (the gardener and handyman), and at least one maid lived at the Kilns along with dogs and cats. There were also frequent visitors.

A renowned and avid walker, Lewis trekked regularly from his rooms at Magdalen College to his home at the Kilns. According to Hooper, "Lewis thought nothing of walking out of his college to his home—that's four miles—picking up a walking stick at that point, and then going for a walk. He'd come back to the Kilns and have tea, after which he'd walk back to the college. He loved walking."

Lewis also took frequent walks in the rolling hills west of Oxford known as the Cotswolds. "He loved the Cotswolds and England's lake country as well as Northern Ireland, where he grew up," said Hart. "And he certainly loved taking walking tours. His imagination was nurtured by the beauty of the countryside."

"I think Jack would have been very bored if he lived somewhere where the climate never changed," said Gresham. "He enjoyed the ebullient expressions of God's creativity that we find in the world— mountains and forests. Jack loved the animals, the trees, the hedgerows, the shrubs, the plants. He enjoyed a blustering, boisterous rainstorm, a good snowfall, a hard frost. But he saw nature as an expression of God more than as something symbolic of God."

While living at the Kilns and teaching at Oxford (and later at Cambridge), Lewis entered the busiest and most prolific time of his life. As Hooper remarked in the previous chapter, Lewis now had "something to say" and he was clearly intent on saying it.

In 1933, Lewis began a remarkable publishing spree beginning with *The Pilgrim's Regress: An Allegorical Apology for Christianity, Reason and Romanticism* (1933). Following it were *The Allegory of Love: A Study in Medieval Tradition* (1936); his first science-fiction book in what would become a trilogy, *Out of the Silent Planet* (1938); *The Problem of Pain* (1940); *The Screwtape Letters* (1942); *Perelandra*, second in the trilogy (1943); *That Hideous Strength*, third in the trilogy (1945); *The Great Divorce* (1945); and *Miracles* (1947). In 1950, Lewis published *The Lion, the Witch and the Wardrobe*, the first of seven children's books in the The Chronicles of Narnia series. The other six Narnia books penned by Lewis were published between 1952 and 1956. In 1952, Lewis published what many consider his most enduring

Christian book: *Mere Christianity*. His autobiography, *Surprised by Joy*, was released in 1955. *Till We Have Faces: A Myth Retold*, which Lewis considered his best book, was published in 1956. *The Four Loves* was released in 1960. In 1961, Lewis published *A Grief Observed* under the pen name N. W. Clerk. His last book, *Letters to Malcolm: Chiefly on Prayer*, was published posthumously in 1964.

It's impossible to know how Lewis was able to accomplish such a prolific writing feat. Lewis conceived of and wrote an incredible and diverse volume of work while seated at his tiny desk in the Kilns and in his rooms at Magdalen College. He did it while maintaining his own studies. He did it while serving the needs of Mrs. Moore and her daughter. He did it against the backdrop of World War II. He did it while coping with the drinking problems faced by his brother. And he did it while continuing his work as a teacher at one of the world's leading universities. For years, students and readers of Lewis's work have been impressed by the abundance of his writings as well as his work habits. They've also been curious as to the source of his inspiration.

"Lewis was one of those people who could write in the oddest circumstances," said Hooper. "To Lewis, writing and thinking were almost the same thing. His thoughts became crystal-clear only when he wrote them down. He could break off from looking after somebody and then go and write a chapter. He could write at odd moments. He could write standing up or while riding on a train."

Lewis emphasized the art of writing as well as the content. "Lewis found that he always whispered words aloud when he was writing because, he told me, 'it's as important to please the

"I think he had a sense in which
the fiction wasn't written by him, it was
written by something else. He was given
the images, he was given the lion, which
came jumping into his dreams, or rather
his nightmares, in 1947 or thereabouts.
It made him write the stories. He said,
'After I had written the first,
Aslan wrote the rest.'"

—COLIN MANLOVE

ear as it is the eye,'" continued Hooper. "If you pick up a nib pen
and try it, you find that it gives you just the rhythm you need.
Because by the time you've written about seven words, you need
to pause and think about what you're going to say. So you dip
the pen in the ink and you start writing again. It's a beautiful
rhythm and it worked for Lewis."

"He would get up early in the morning, go to his work, and
when pupils came in, he already had been scratching away at
something for an hour," said Manlove. "He might have been

marking an essay or composing a book. As far as speed is concerned, people were astounded at the speed with which he produced the Narnia books. *The Silver Chair*, for example, was written in a couple of months."

Hart added, "He didn't talk much about his own writing process. He did write several essays on writing for children and on why he chose the fairy-tale form when he started writing The Chronicles of Narnia. But he didn't talk a lot about his own specific inspiration for the various books he wrote. As a lecturer, an essayist, and a writer of literary criticism, he wrote about other people's books. He didn't write a lot about his own."

"Who and what inspired C. S. Lewis in his writings is a very complex question," said Hooper. "Most of all, I think he was given things to say by God. He said, 'I never exactly made a book. It's rather like taking dictation. I was given things to say.' As for people who inspired him, you'll never get to the end of that. There were people like Tolkien who were very important to him because they discussed writing and discussed the things they were writing about. As far as inspiration is concerned, most of Lewis's books came to him through visual things. *The Lion, the Witch and the Wardrobe* started with a faun in a snowy wood with an umbrella. He saw a magnificent queen on a sled. Then later Aslan the lion came into it. Something always bubbled up in Lewis's mind."

"He had an active imagination," said Mitchell. "He experienced a lot through reading and through the eyes of other people, or through the experiences of other people as they were expressed and articulated in the books that he read. He listened with his eyes and he listened with his ears. The other thing is that Lewis believed that his experience was not something unique—that much of it was common to the ordinary individual. So when he takes a walk and there's this moment when the wind whips up, and that poignant smell of autumnness comes to him and the leaves blow in a certain way, he said, 'I'm not the only one who's experienced that.'"

"I think he had a sense in which the fiction wasn't written by him, it was written by something else," said Manlove. "He was given the images, he was given the lion, which came jumping into his dreams, or rather his nightmares, in 1947 or thereabouts. It made him write the stories. He said, 'After I had written the first, Aslan wrote the rest.'"

According to Gresham, "I'm not sure that Jack ever sat down and said to himself, 'I will now teach Christianity through children's literature.' I don't think it happened that way at all. And as I've said before and will probably say many times again, while Jack was the writer of *The Lion, the Witch and the Wardrobe*, the Holy Spirit of God was its author."

Many writers call the source of their inspiration the "muse." It is, literally, an outside force or spirit that ignites one's imagination. "I have a feeling that Lewis would say that muses were the early imagination's way of expressing something," said Hart. "The idea became more clear with the Christian understanding of the Holy Spirit. The muses were the link between divine power and ordinary human beings. In other words, the muses were fundamentally true."

"I think the Spirit inspired him once his imagination and his mind were transformed by Christ," said Dorsett. "He was a midlife convert when he became a Christian and he was inspired to communicate Christian things. Lewis had an unusual gift. He understood the power of story and he knew that when we enter into a story, we enter into another world. But we also connect our own story to it. Of course, Lewis leads us to the greatest story ever told."

During the early part of World War II, Lewis was impacted by the pain and struggle that besieged England and all of Europe. At that time, the editor of a popular book series called The Christian Challenge series commissioned Lewis to write a book on pain and suffering. The result, *The Problem of Pain*, was published in October 1940. It became an immediate bestseller in England and eventually grew popular in the United States.

The book's popularity grew from Lewis's ability to ask the universal question: If God is good and all-powerful, then why does he allow his creatures to suffer pain? In *The Problem of Pain*, Lewis answered from his own Christian perspective. Lewis wrote:

> Pain is unmasked, unmistakable evil; every man knows that something is wrong when he is being hurt . . . pain is not only immediately recognisable evil, but evil impossible to ignore. We can

"One of the things that came
through in his writing is that the
problem of pain is a mystery. We can't fully
understand it, but we trust God because we
know God's character as he revealed it to us
through Jesus Christ. The Scriptures reveal
to us the problem of evil and the problem
of pain as well as the character of God.
They also reveal that there is a freedom
in humanity to make choices."

—LYLE DORSETT

rest contentedly in our sins and in our stupidities; and anyone who has watched gluttons shovelling down the most exquisite foods as if they did not know what they were eating, will admit that we can ignore even pleasure. But pain insists upon being attended to. God whispers to us in our pleasures, speaks in our conscience, but shouts in our pain: it is His megaphone to rouse a deaf world.[1]

The Problem of Pain was really his first Christian apologetic work," said Mitchell. "It tackles one of the biggest issues facing humanity, and not only for Christianity but for any religious faith. It's not necessarily an easy read, but a layperson can read it and understand it. It put Lewis on the map as a defender of the Christian faith."

"One of the big questions everybody wrestles with is, Why is there pain in the world? Why evil?" said Dorsett. "What do we do with the problem of evil? What do we do with the problem of pain if there is a God? How do we explain it if there's a God and if God is good? If he is omnipotent, how come there's evil in the world? There are no simple answers to those questions, but I do think that one of the themes that ties a lot of Lewis's writings together is that he's wrestling with that.

"One of the things that came through in his writing is that the problem of pain is a mystery. We can't fully understand it, but we trust God because we know God's character as he revealed it to us through Jesus Christ. The Scriptures reveal to us the problem of evil and the problem of pain as well as the character of God They also reveal that there is a freedom in humanity to make choices.

"Lewis saw pain coming from a variety of levels for a variety of reasons," continued Dorsett. "There's pain that comes upon us when we sin, when we deliberately disobey God, or we disobey God without even knowing it. The sin brings pain. Lewis says that God can whisper to us when things are going well, but that in our pain he screams at us. He yells so that we can really hear him when we're in pain. There's pain that comes from God trying to fashion us and shape us. There's pain that comes from sinfulness that we've done to ourselves. But there's also pain that just happens to people, that comes from the outside through such things as war. But the issue isn't, Why do we have pain? The issue is, What do we do with it? What do we let God do in the midst of it? That's the issue. But finally, as Lewis understood and as the Christian faith teaches, God will redeem even the most horrid things for his glory. Christ's horrid death on the cross became the act that saved humankind. So we have a God that knows pain. He's suffered with us in our pain."

CHAPTER FIVE

SCREWTAPE
AND THE
SOCRATIC CLUB

*N*ot long after he'd completed *The Problem of Pain*, Lewis was attending a midday service at his local parish when he was struck by an idea. Why not write from an entirely new perspective, using satire as a tool for instruction and insight? Why not write a series of letters of advice from a senior devil to his apprentice? Lewis's brainstorm resulted in what was for years his most popular book: *The Screwtape Letters*.

Lewis wrote *The Screwtape Letters* very quickly and by February 1941, all thirty-one letters that comprised the manuscript were completed. Thanks to a serialization in a Church of England weekly called the *Guardian*, the senior devil, Screwtape, and his apprentice, Wormwood, were soon household names in England.

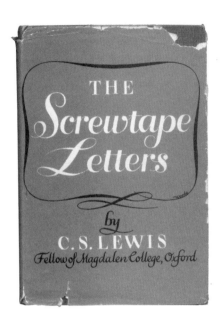

The *Guardian*, the only newspaper to which Lewis subscribed at the time, paid him approximately $1,500 for the entire series. Lewis donated the money to charity.

When the letters were published as a book in February 1942, the first printing of two thousand copies sold out before the book appeared on store shelves. By the end of the year, *The Screwtape Letters* had been reprinted eight times and its success had carried across the Atlantic to America. Well received by critics, *The Screwtape Letters* was considered a wildly entertaining satire that, because of its humorous dealings with the temptation of average men and women (the "patients"), as seen from a devil's point of view, appealed to both the secular and nonsecular audiences.

"One way to describe *The Screwtape Letters*," said Mitchell, "is that the book stands things on their head. That which we normally consider bad becomes good and vice versa. God becomes the enemy. Satan is the good figure. As Screwtape tutors his nephew, Wormwood, we see things through their eyes as demonic agents. Selfishness, self-centeredness, and destroying people become good things. Everything becomes the opposite of the way we know it.

What Lewis is trying to do is reveal something universal about the human experience. It's funny, and it's tragic."

In Letter 6, for example, Screwtape tells Wormwood:

There is nothing like suspense and anxiety for barricading a human's mind against the Enemy [God]. He wants men to be concerned with what they do; our business is to keep them thinking about what will happen to them.

Your patient will, of course, have picked up the notion that he must submit with patience to the Enemy's will. What the Enemy means by this is primarily that he should accept with patience the tribulation which has actually been dealt out to him— the present anxiety and suspense. It is about *this* that he is to say, "Thy will be done," and for the daily task of bearing this that the daily bread will be provided.[1]

In Letter 18, Screwtape begins his letter to Wormwood:

Even under Slubgob you must have learned at college the routine technique of sexual temptation, and since, for us spirits, this whole subject is one of considerable tedium (though a necessary part of our training), I will pass it over. But on the larger issues involved I think you have a good deal to learn.

The Enemy's demand on humans takes the form of a dilemma; either complete abstinence or unmitigated monogamy. Ever since our Father's first great victory, we have rendered the former very difficult to them. The latter, for the last few centuries, we have been closing up as a way of escape. We have done this through the poets and novelists by persuading the humans that a curious, and usually shortlived, experience which they call "being in love" is the only respectable ground for marriage; that marriage can, and ought to, render this excitement permanent; and that a marriage which does not do so is no longer binding. This idea is our parody of an idea that came from the Enemy.[2]

Both Christians and non-Christians found *Screwtape* a pivotal and entertaining read. "I love this book because it was instrumental in my own conversion," affirmed Dorsett. "Lewis wanted to write a book where he talked about the reality of evil, the reality of Satan, the reality of the demonic presence in the world. He wanted to do something that would engage people's imaginations as well as their minds. So he settled on the technique of these letters where the senior demon tells his nephew how they're going to tempt people who belong to the 'Enemy.' In other words, those who follow God. The demonic forces don't know everything, they can't be everywhere, they don't have all power. But they're very potent and very effective. He tries to show what lines they push, where they work, what are the things that bother them, and what they can't understand. For example, they can't understand pure love."

Not everyone loved the concept. "Tolkien was very upset with Lewis that he dedicated *The Screwtape Letters* to him," continued Dorsett. "He said, 'Jack, you have no business writing books like that because you're neither ordained nor a theologian.' And Lewis said, 'I wish I didn't have to, but until the theologians and ordained clergy begin to communicate with ordinary people in the vernacular, in a way that they can understand, I'm going to have to do this kind of thing.' Lewis's genius was putting Christian truth and Christian doctrine into the vernacular."

Years after *Screwtape*'s publication, many would argue that Lewis was right. The book's success, due in large part to its humor and the simplified approach, speaks volumes.

"If I were asked what was his most important work in terms of conversion power, I would say *The Screwtape Letters* without hesitation," said Manlove.

TIME MAGAZINE, SEPTEMBER 1947.

"He wrote in such a way that people could identify with the temptations described in the book. They knew what it was like to have these petty envies, rages, prides, and whatnot, which Lewis analyzed chapter by chapter."

"The letters cover the whole gamut of human life," added Hooper. "Most of the temptations, they're wonderful. They're brilliant. As you read them you just fall about laughing. But part of your laughter is the fact that you see the point."

"Tolkien was very upset with Lewis
that he dedicated *The Screwtape Letters* to
him. He said, 'Jack, you have no business
writing books like that because you're neither
ordained nor a theologian.' And Lewis said,
'I wish I didn't have to, but until the
theologians and ordained clergy begin
to communicate with ordinary people
in the vernacular, in a way that they can
understand, I'm going to have to do this
kind of thing.' Lewis's genius was
putting Christian truth and Christian
doctrine into the vernacular."

—LYLE DORSETT

Gresham added, "*The Screwtape Letters* is a wonderful guide on the nature of temptation and how to combat it. It's a book of instruction, interest, amusement, delight. There are so many depths in it.

"Interestingly, Jack found it one of the easiest books to write, but also one of the most unpleasant," continued Gresham. "He had to do a sort of mental gear change to think like the Enemy. And he found it a grubby, dirtying process. But the frightening thing to him was that as soon as he'd done so, the ability to tempt seemed to be so easy. It disconcerted him. The great lesson, of course, is that you never find out how strong temptation can be by giving in to it; all you discover is your own level of weakness. You don't find out how strong temptation can be until you've successfully resisted it."

Published against the backdrop of Nazism and World War II, *The Screwtape Letters* put Lewis and his work on the world stage. In 1947, a caricature of Lewis with a pitchfork-wielding devil situated behind him appeared on the cover of *Time* magazine. It was a rare and unusual occurrence for an Oxford don.

Another major development occurred in Lewis's life during January 1942, when he became president of the Oxford Socratic Club. Conceived as a discussion group comprised of both believers and nonbelievers on matters of faith and religion, the Socratic Club was the idea of a pastoral advisor named Stella Aldwinckle. Because of Lewis's reputation and argumentative skills, Aldwinckle asked him to be president. Meetings were held every other Monday night and the club soon became extremely popular among undergraduate students. As many as eighty to one hundred students attended regularly during Lewis's tenure as president from 1942 to 1954.

Many in the club considered Lewis bombastic in his attacks on nonbelievers. As a result of his vociferous role in defense of Christianity, Lewis, it may be argued, fostered a division between his beliefs and those of many agnostic scholars. He frequently used the Monday night meetings to square off against invited lecturers who were considered among the best minds in England at the time.

"One of the more important roles that Lewis played in his life as a Christian was as the president of the Socratic Club," said Mitchell, who has authored significant work on Lewis's role in the Socratic Club. "During his tenure there were well over two hundred meetings with about 113 or so different participants. They were the best in their fields from across all disciplines—history, English, philosophy, literature, sciences. And the basic agenda involved having a Christian or non-Christian come forth and deliver a paper. Once that was done, the meeting was opened up to discussion among the people who attended."

The Socratic Club was the perfect forum for Lewis's strengths as a debater, honed years earlier under the tutelage of William Kirkpatrick. The skills he'd learned as a young intellectual not only helped him prepare for entrance to Oxford, they also served him well when squaring off against the secular scholars poised to refute his arguments.

"One of the key aspects of that training was the two to three years he spent with William T. Kirkpatrick," said Mitchell. "He'd been trained not only in the classics but also in what is called dialectic—the art of argumentation. Kirkpatrick was really an

"He believed that if Christianity
were true, then, over the long haul,
it would prove itself to have the intellectual
fiber and muscle to persevere. The reason he
was in the Socratic Club was because he felt
the Christian understanding of reality in the
world was the truth and was worth putting
out there publicly. It was worth the risk of
being shown up at times in the debate arena.
He tried to demonstrate that Christianity
wasn't this feeble, weak-minded
understanding of reality."

—CHRISTOPHER W. MITCHELL

expert in that area. He walked it and talked it. All of his encounters with Lewis had some sort of dialectic involved. In the beginning, Lewis was not equal to it. But as Lewis expresses in *Surprised by Joy*, near the end of his time with Kirkpatrick, he had pretty well mastered it. He went to Oxford fully armed, and the Socratic

Club was tailor-made for him. He came with the certainty and surety of his faith in an intellectual arena, a neutral arena where both sides had the opportunity to bring their arguments to bear."

"Kirkpatrick was an atheist, or at least an n-degree agnostic," said Dorsett. "But what Kirkpatrick did was to teach Lewis to think. Lewis had a brilliant mind but it had never really been disciplined before his study with Kirkpatrick. He taught him how to read in new ways. He taught him how to think critically and how to speak clearly and effectively. He taught him how to be precise."

Mitchell contends, "Lewis saw the Socratic Club as vitally important to the intellectual health of Christianity. It needed a forum where the fate of the intellectual side could be put forth. And what was unique about it was that the Christians initiated this arena, not the unbelieving world. Believers were the ones who put themselves out there. Lewis didn't think they would always come out on top, because intellectual argument finally won. But if their arguments were good and sound, fine. It didn't mean he didn't believe in Christianity. Rather, it meant that sometimes Christians didn't argue as persuasively as the opponents. In fact, in 1954, Lewis wrote to his friend Don Bebe Griffiths and said, 'They often wipe the floor with us at the Socratic Club.' He knew they didn't always come out on top.

"But Lewis believed in the enterprise. He believed that if Christianity were true, then, over the long haul, it would prove itself to have the intellectual fiber and muscle to persevere," continued Mitchell. "The reason he was in the Socratic Club was because he felt the Christian understanding of reality in the world was the truth and was worth putting out there publicly. It was worth the risk of being shown up at times in the debate arena. He tried to demonstrate that Christianity wasn't this feeble, weak-minded understanding of reality."

Lewis continued as president of the Socratic Club until his departure from Oxford University in 1954.

CHAPTER SIX

MERELY CHRISTIAN

*N*ot long after Lewis had completed *The Screwtape Letters*, Dr. James Welch, director of religious programming for BBC radio, contacted him with a request for help. In response, during August 1941, Lewis began a series of four fifteen-minute broadcasts on Christianity called *Right and Wrong: A Clue to the Meaning of the Universe*. Lewis hoped to engage listeners by talking about the laws of nature, or what he called "objective right and wrong."

The success of the first series led to a sequel called *What Christians Believe*. In the second series, Lewis acknowledged the beliefs that are common to all Christians—in other words, the shared convictions that exist beyond denominational Christianity.

The two lecture series were then combined and published in July 1942 in a book called *Broadcast Talks*. It became an immediate bestseller, and, along with the broadcasts themselves, contributed to Lewis's growing notoriety in England. A third radio series soon followed. Entitled *Christian Behaviour*, the talks provided an analysis of the Christian values and virtues in which Lewis believed. Several of the talks were also recorded under the title *Beyond Personality: The Christian Idea of God* (or *First Steps in the Doctrine of the Trinity*). They remain for sale today.

Shortly after the first set of talks was broadcast, Lewis began a series of regular lectures to Britain's Royal Air Force as part of his contribution to the war effort. Because of the success of *The Screwtape Letters* and the radio broadcasts, Lewis received countless letters from people wanting to share their own insights and seeking his advice and spiritual guidance. With the help of Warnie, who was now filling more and more of a secretarial role for Lewis, he attempted to respond to all who wrote.

Could Lewis have anticipated the popularity of his radio broadcasts and the inquiries from listeners and readers seeking his insights into faith? It's not likely. But it may have led to his decision to combine three of his lectures into one book, the 1952 publication *Mere Christianity*.

"I think the basis of his widespread popularity is that his Christian faith was, as he called it, 'mere Christianity,'" said Dabney Hart. "It was basic Christianity. It was Christianity that created a unifying element."

"I'm not sure it's universally appealing," said Lyle Dorsett, "but it appeals to a certain type of person. It's a book for people who have honest questions, people who are grappling with a lot of issues. Lewis was trying to communicate that there's a transformational relationship that takes place between the soul of the man or woman and God when the Spirit comes in. Philosophically speaking, Lewis was writing a book in an age when naturalism and materialism was the reigning mind-set, the reigning spirit of the times. So he tried to take things on in a very logical fashion and explain that 'here is basic Christianity. Here's what it really looks like.'

"What do you do with a world full of people who say Jesus was a great teacher?" continued Dorsett. "Yet they're also saying he was not who he said he was. He was a great teacher but he's not God. Well, along came Lewis, who said, 'How can he be a great man, a great teacher, and a wonderful prophet but not be who he says he is? He's either a liar, he's a lunatic, or he is who he says he is.'"

"Many readers come to C. S. Lewis because they are Christian seekers and a friend recommends *Mere Christianity*," added Hart. "And I think those readers of C. S. Lewis find that he's able to explain concepts that have been obscure or rigidly dogmatic in a way that they can understand and relate to their own experience. They find, for the first time, someone who's writing about Christian doctrine who is clear and often even amusing, and ultimately very convincing. They also find that Lewis is strikingly different from other Christian authors they've read in that he's never anything that could be called pious. He's serious, and at the same time he's lighthearted because he has great joy in everything he has to say about the faith."

"Mere Christianity," according to Lewis, does not include sects, divisions, and denominations. Despite the role that J. R. R. Tolkien,

HOLY TRINITY CHURCH, HEADINGTON QUARRY, OXFORD.

a Catholic, had played in his conversion to Christianity, Lewis's expression and celebration of joy in his faith resulted in his being merely Christian and not denominational. Even his own choice in churches (which for him was an Anglican church called Holy Trinity Church in Headington) was, according to Douglas Gresham, made based on its proximity to his home at the Kilns. Walter Hooper added, "It's a beautiful nineteenth-century church, a very picturesque church. But it wasn't so much Lewis's choice, it was just his church. In England, if you live in a parish, it's expected that you will go to the parish church."

For many non-Christians who are exposed to the Christian world, the denominational aspects of Christianity can be confusing, may seem divisive, and for some, can even detract from what Christians believe is the authenticity and truth of their faith. Lewis was able to do more than simplify the concepts of Christianity for a newcomer. He was able to create a work that gets at the core of what all Christians share: a belief in Jesus Christ as the Son of God. For a man raised in Ireland and

> "[Readers] find that Lewis is strikingly different from other Christian authors they've read in that he's never anything that could be called pious. He's serious, and at the same time he's lighthearted because he has great joy in everything he has to say about the faith."
>
> —DABNEY HART

England, two nations where the lines between Catholicism and Protestantism have for centuries created division in social, intellectual, and political worlds, Lewis was able to share a unifying vision of his faith.

"The fact that Jack's work as a Christian apologist and writer is so well accepted across the denominational spectrum is because it doesn't deal with anything denominational," said Gresham. "He avoided denominational issues because he found them to be so trivial. He found that what we have in common is so much more important than the differences that separate us. I believe that one of the greatest problems with denominational churches is that they tend to concentrate on the trivial at the cost of the essential. I think this is a sadness in Christendom. Jack obviously felt much the same way. 'Mere Christianity' is the important part. Toward the end of his life, Jack was moving closer to Christ and farther from any denominational lines at all."

In the preface to *Mere Christianity*, Lewis described his perspective clearly:

> The reader should be warned that I offer no help to anyone who is hesitating between two Christian "denominations." You will not learn from me whether you ought to become an Anglican, a Methodist, a Presbyterian, or a Roman Catholic. This omission is intentional (even in the list I have just given the order is alphabetical). There is no mystery about my position. I am a very ordinary layman of the Church of England, not especially "high," nor especially "low," nor especially anything else. But in this book I am not trying to convert anyone to my own position. Ever since I became a Christian I have thought that the best, perhaps the only, service I could do for my unbelieving neighbours was to explain and defend the belief that has been common to nearly all Christians at all times. I had more than one reason for thinking this. In the first place, the questions which divide Christians from one another often involve points of high Theology or even of ecclesiastical history, which ought never to be treated except by real experts. I should have been out of my depth in such waters: more in need of help myself than able to help others. And secondly, I think we must admit that the discussion of these disputed points has no tendency at all to bring an outsider into the Christian fold.[1]

Lewis also wrote: *"I am not writing to expound something I could call 'my religion,' but to expound 'mere' Christianity, which is what it is and what it was long before I was born."*[2]

Mere Christianity is filled with passages that define Christianity in its simplicity and in the commonality of shared belief that has been compromised by both Christians and non-Christians during the past two millennia, including: *"We are told that Christ was killed for us, that His death has washed out our sins, and that by dying He disabled death itself. That is the formula. That is Christianity. That is what has to be believed."* Lewis also wrote: *"The central Christian belief is that Christ's death has somehow put us right with God and given us a fresh start."*[3]

"I think Lewis was a realist and knew we'd always have these denominational distinctions, but he believed in 'mere Christianity,'" said Mitchell. "And the illustration he used in the book to explain it is the idea of a hallway with many doors. And the hallway that is common to all the doors of all the rooms is 'mere Christianity.' And then out of that hallway you have different doors. There's a door that goes into a Catholic church, and probably within that door you have some other doors for different sorts of schools of thought within Roman Catholicism. There's the Protestant door for Presbyterians and Baptists and so on. But we all have this common hallway.

"Lewis was saying that there's a common theological, doctrinal tradition that runs through all the major Christian traditions," continued Mitchell. "The Greek Orthodox tradition, the Roman Catholic tradition, and the Protestant tradition—they all hold to

LEWIS DURING AN INTERVIEW, 1946.

a Trinitarian conception of God. They all hold to the Son of God becoming incarnate at a particular point in history and being incarnate for the purpose of our salvation. The focus of that is most poignant on the cross, but it really begins from the time of conception all the way to that point. Indeed, it's God dying on that cross for us in human flesh, and not just appearing in human flesh, but a real incarnation—the mystery that God actually became a human being. It's not an Eastern conception of Maya and illusion, it's a real incarnation, and this one is the Savior of all mankind, whether we recognize it or not. It's at this point, and only at this point, that God becomes incarnate and performs this redemptive work. And this redemptive work involved sacrifice and suffering. And out of that come redemption and healing. And ultimately at the end is the consummation of the ages, which involves judgment and redemption. All of those are held on to.

"Now, in terms of Christ's work on the cross, which is viewed normally as the concept of atonement, all agree that the Atonement was a covering for sin. How that was accomplished is where the differences come in. And Lewis recognized those differences, but what he dealt with was the concept of atonement itself. He believed that Christ dealt with our sins in a way that allowed God to accept us. They're no longer a barrier in our relationship to God. That's reality. All Christianity, from the first century to the present, believes that. There's this common tradition. Lewis was seeking to identify those elements that are common to all the major traditions of Christianity." Together, all denominations form the "hallway" of shared Christian faith.

Gresham added, "*Mere Christianity* cuts through all the denominational rubbish, all the dross that we've added to what Christ did, and what Christ taught. It cuts through right to the nitty-gritty of the matter and makes it so very simple for people to understand what Jesus was really all about. It's very important that we get away from all the groupings of people that have decided to add little bits on to the gospel, here and there, and as a result have come up with a liturgy and doctrine that don't actually dovetail with the Scriptures. What Jack did was to get us back to what Jesus taught, the simple truth, and to make that as simple and as acceptable as he possibly could. Underneath it is the most beautiful truth the world has ever seen. *Mere Christianity* draws back that dark curtain that people try to draw across the blinding face of God."

"He writes as a person who was himself infected by this," said Hooper. "He was glad that God came down to earth and saved us."

"Lewis was seeking to translate the thinking and teaching of the church, this basic theology, and serve it up in a way in which the common person could understand and appreciate it, and make an intelligent decision as to whether to embrace it or not embrace it," said Mitchell. "He wanted to identify that to which all Christians could say, 'Yes.' Today, people are wanting to break away from that longstanding tradition. Lewis would say that once you break away from that, you're outside the loop, you're outside what's been considered Christianity. So, should women be ordained or not ordained? Lewis would say that's not part of 'mere Christianity.' But if you say, 'All that Jesus was doing on the cross was a good illustration—he wasn't really doing anything about our sins,' then Lewis would say that's outside the bounds of 'mere Christianity.'"

"Jack cut away all the peripheral, nonessential bits and left the

"Mere Christianity cuts through all
the denominational rubbish, all the dross
that we've added to what Christ did, and
what Christ taught. It cuts through right to
the nitty-gritty of the matter and makes it
so very simple for people to understand
what Jesus was really all about."

—DOUGLAS GRESHAM

glowing core," said Gresham. "If you follow what Christ taught
and you preach what Christ taught, then people will come to the
church. If you don't, they won't."

"There are certain more fundamentalist-minded Protestants
that have a hard time with Lewis, especially because of certain
lifestyle issues such as his drinking and smoking," said Mitchell,
"and also some who would be against what they would call certain
'magical' elements within his writing. But with the exception of
those, which are really few, Lewis has an incredibly broad appeal
and I think it's because he stayed with 'mere Christianity.' He dealt
with those things that were common to the faith. He wrote well
and in an engaging way. He clarified issues and appealed to a
common tradition. I think, generally, that Christians aren't happy

about the divisions. They want a reason to believe that the divisions aren't as big as we make them out to be. Especially for the common person, the common Christian, Lewis was able to say, 'Wow, there is something bigger than my denomination. There is this thing called "mere Christianity."'"

There are, of course, sects and denominational differences in many of the world's leading religious and spiritual practices, from Theravada, Zen and Tantric Buddhism, and Sunni and Shiite Islam to the mystical practices of Sufis. Judaism is filled with distinctions among its believers, and the practice of Hinduism in Bali is distinctly different from that practiced in India. In Christianity, the differences in religious practice vary so widely that many outside the faith have trouble discerning the common ground between Greek Orthodoxy, Catholicism, Coptic Christianity, and the various denominations of the Protestant world such as Methodists, Baptists, Lutherans, Episcopalians, Anglicans, Unitarians, and Mennonites (to name a few). What Lewis was able to do with *Mere Christianity* was to bring believers back to one unifying element. And in so doing, he opened a door for readers and seekers from all parts of the world.

CHAPTER SEVEN

THE MAGIC NEVER ENDS

*H*itler's bombs began falling on London in 1940. Though Oxford and the surrounding areas were relatively safe by comparison, the impact of World War II was still significant. Many basic resources were rationed and blackout curtains had to be placed over the windows each evening to deter potential air strikes. Residents learned to live with a measure of fear. As a veteran, Lewis did what he could for the war effort, including (with Mrs. Moore's assistance) volunteering the Kilns as a home for children evacuated from coastal cities that were vulnerable to German attack.

It can be argued that *The Problem of Pain, The Screwtape Letters,* and the essays that eventually comprised *Mere Christianity* were impacted by the war and its related moral issues. But with children now living at the Kilns, the seeds were also planted for what may be Lewis's most well-known and universally ap-pealing work. It began when one of the children asked Lewis if she could climb inside a freestanding wooden wardrobe he had in the house. She also asked him whether there was anything behind it.

Although he'd never written for children, Lewis found that the young girl's request inspired his imagination and his love of fantasy. Ten years later, Lewis published his first book in The Chronicles of Narnia series: *The Lion, the Witch and the Wardrobe.*

According to Manlove, "Lewis said, 'Did I think of writing for a child? Never. Think of writing for a child and you're dead, more or less. You just became a commercial hack.' His view was: 'I wrote children's books because that seemed to be the sort of books I felt I must write.' I also believe he wrote them because he himself found childhood, at that particular point of his life, absolutely crucial to him. I actually believe Lewis saw children and childhood as a way of realizing or re-creating his own faith. That's what he does in *The Lion, the Witch and the Wardrobe.* There are four children who are enthroned by the end and I think they're actually enthroned in Lewis himself—the frozen spirit of C. S. Lewis was thawed out into spring."

"No one was writing children's literature the way he thought it should be written," added Gresham. "The Chronicles of Narnia are a collection of seven books that fall into the genre of fairy tales, though they're much richer than the average fairy tale.

They're books about another world, another continuum altogether, which you can't get to from here, except by magic."

In *The Lion, the Witch and the Wardrobe,* four siblings visit the house of old Professor Kirke. Early in the story the youngest girl, Lucy, climbs through the professor's wardrobe and finds herself in the mythical land of Narnia. Eventually the others follow and while there, they encounter an evil witch and a powerful but loving lion named Aslan.

"Narnia is a universe unto its own," said Manlove. "It has its own little countries, Archenland and Calormen and so on, that are quite separate from ours. It's a place that's like a person because it ages. Throughout the books, Narnia gets older and more decrepit and finally, in the last book, it literally becomes geriatric and drops to pieces. It's a very permeable country. I always feel that there are all these people coming in and out. It's like a big sort of national cheese grater."

"We discover Narnia in the first of the seven books, which is *The Magician's Nephew,*" said Gresham. "We see the world, Narnia, created by Aslan. He gives its inhabitants the gift of free will, speech, sapience, and so on. And two children from our world get there by the works of a peddling little magician in Victorian England who is trying to work magic. And they have an adventure. The second book is set during World War II, when the children are evacuated from London and find themselves in a mysterious old mansion and, again, stumble into Narnia. And they discover that a thousand years have passed since the first children visited.

"The time line of Narnia has no relationship with the time line

"[The Chronicles of Narnia]
are, perhaps, the greatest classics of
children's literature of the twentieth century.
I think one of the reasons for that is that
they deal with inescapable truth. They
deal with reconciliation, forgiveness,
things of that nature that are essential
for children to learn about at some point
in their development. I don't care whether
someone is an atheist or a Buddhist or
what, children should still read The
Chronicles of Narnia because of the
very moral teaching they get from reading
them, and the great fun they will have."

—DOUGLAS GRESHAM

of our world at all," continued Gresham. "And children from our world keep going to Narnia and having fantastic and fascinating adventures with all sorts of interesting characters—fauns and centaurs. And the animals of Narnia are much larger than they are here and are gifted with speech and thought. So there are badgers and beavers and people like that—and they *are* people. It's a fascinating mixture of all kinds of cultural and mythological entities and ideas. But underlying them all is this strong ethical and moral message in each book. And of course, *The Lion, the Witch and the Wardrobe* is a sort of representational picture of what God might do if there were a world in which the animals were the people and could talk, and God had to save that world in much the same way he has to save this one."

While *The Lion, the Witch and the Wardrobe* is the most popular of the books in the series and was written first, it's not first in the chronology of the series. "I don't think Jack set about to write the Narnia chronicles in the order in which they were eventually written," said Gresham. "He wrote *The Lion, the Witch and the Wardrobe* first and then realized, having written several others, that he needed to explain where this world had come from, how it came into existence in the first place.

"I suspect that by the time he wrote *The Magician's Nephew*, which is about the creation of Narnia, he had already envisaged writing *The Last Battle*, which is about the eventual destruction of Narnia and the creation of the 'True Narnia.' Which explains why the world in which we live is a mere shadow of that which we are to go on to. True life hasn't begun yet and death itself is an illusion. And all those philosophical concepts are contained in these seven books.

"They are, perhaps, the greatest classics of children's literature of the twentieth century," continued Gresham. "I think one of the reasons for that is that they deal with inescapable truth. They deal with reconciliation, forgiveness, things of that nature that are essential for children to learn about at some point in their development. I don't care whether someone is an atheist or a Buddhist or what, children should still read The Chronicles of Narnia because of the very moral teaching they get from reading them, and the great fun they will have."

Lewis biographer George Sayer agrees:

> The Narnia stories show a complete acceptance of the Tao, of the conventional and traditional moral code. Humanity, courage, loyalty, honesty, kindness, and unselfishness are virtues. Children who might perhaps object to the code if they were taught it in churches and schools accept it easily and naturally when they see it practiced by the characters they love. They are learning morality in the best and perhaps only effective way.[1]

Lewis himself saw the tales as offering more than moral lessons. "Lewis called the Narnian chronicles 'pre-evangelism,'" said Dorsett. "They awaken people's imaginations to the reality of a spiritual world. He's showing us that yes, there are light and darkness. There is a struggle for good and evil and it's very personal. But there's always hope in it."

With all that can be read into The Chronicles of Narnia, the great strength of the series is its ability to entertain young people and their parents with magical, epic stories based on conflicts between good and evil characters. Both secular and nonsecular readers value the series, and many children and parents read The Chronicles of Narnia in its entirety without ever knowing about Lewis's connection to the Christian faith or the Christian underpinnings of the work.

"Lewis would say it didn't matter," said Manlove, "because as long as you've got the rhythm right, that's all that counts. He didn't write them as overtly Christian stories. He wrote them so that readers would be surprised at how many resonances his stories occasionally have with the Christian stories we know. What's important are the principles behind the work: the principle of joy versus the principle of abnegation, the current of innocence versus the poison of defamation and desecration. He used to argue that if certain Christian events have happened in this world, they may happen in other worlds as well."

"Let's say God creates another world," said Mitchell. "That is, the same God who created this world creates another one. How might it be played out over there? The morality of The Chronicles of Narnia reflects Judeo-Christian principles. And I think that's why it speaks to so many people who are not Christians, because there's something universal about that kind of morality within our culture."

"Lewis had a whole series of motives he gave for writing, and some of them contradicted one another," said Manlove. "He said, 'I started with images and all I had to do after that was follow what Aslan directed and there was nothing more to it. And as far as any messages are concerned, don't look for them. They're not there.'

And on the other hand, he would say that having written all of this stuff, 'Then I thought, well, I can make use of this somewhere. I can turn it into a Christian purpose or something like that.' But on the whole I think he would have said, 'I've written this material because I liked doing it. I liked writing stories about other worlds, and I liked making adventures. And because I am what I am, they are going to have a certain effect on other people.' Some things were more overtly Christian than others. But I think that he would say it's absolutely worthless to write in order to convert."

"I think Lewis was aware that he would lose people's attention and you'll turn some people off by bringing in Christianity," said Hooper. "And so the Narnia stories are not overtly Christian at all. They don't mention God."

"I can't say that Lewis didn't have an evangelical purpose—that would be absurd," said Manlove. "But he always stated that the evangelical and transformative purpose of his books was not the first one. That is, he wrote and expressed what he was best able to do, then expected that would have its own moral effect without his looking for it. I think he almost assigned it to Aslan."

"People love it because it's magical," said Mitchell. "It touches them. It speaks to them. The Chronicles of Narnia are by far the best-loved and the most widely read of all Lewis's work. And what comes to my mind in terms of my getting around and speaking to people is that it's magical. For those who love The Chronicles of Narnia, it has a place of magic in their life. And I think the idea of re-enchanting life for them is part of it. How it works, I don't know. I just know that it does and the facts speak for themselves. Within the last decades about a million copies are purchased every year. And that's just remarkable, being that it's never been out of print."

Many would agree that The Chronicles of Narnia work because the stories are universal and lasting. But it's more than that. They are simply entertaining. The language Lewis used in the series is fun to read, especially for young people. For example, "If you had to call a badger something, 'Trufflehunter' sounds like a good name to use," said Gresham. "'Nikabrik' for an evil dwarf. 'Trumpkin' for a good dwarf. The names are mostly onomatopoetic—they sound like what they're portraying: 'Glimfeather' for an owl, for example, and 'Puddlegum' the 'marshwiggle.'"

Many mistake the books' subtle Christian parallels as Lewis's attempt to write them as allegory. "They were fantasies," said Dorsett. "They were books for children and they grew out of his imagination. Lewis was inspired to write these, but he didn't set out to say, 'I'm going to communicate the gospel in children's literature.' But that's what happened. A lot of people think that the Narnia chronicles are allegories but they're not, because there's not an exact one-to-one relationship. Aslan is a Christ-like figure, but he's not exactly Christ. The witch is like the Evil One, but not exactly. But clearly anyone who knows the gospel story, or knows Scripture well, encounters it in the Narnia chronicles. Still, someone who is ignorant of Christianity and who knows very little about the doctrines of faith will be taken in by a very powerful story. There's tension, there's intrigue, there are battles, good and evil, the things we're really caught up

in this world. There are human beings who have to make difficult choices, and when they do, they have consequences. It's all
put into a context that even children can understand, and yet
adults are enthralled."

"The stories are so packed with wisdom that you find yourself
learning more about life, the meaning of goodness, badness, and
so on," said Hooper. "But this is not an allegory. This is what
Lewis called a 'supposal.' Suppose there were a world like Narnia.
Suppose it had animals in it. Suppose God wanted to redeem that
world as he has ours. Then suppose he had his Son take on an
earthly form such as a lion and enter this other world as he did
ours. As a reader, you are with Aslan, you hear him, you have
adventures, you ride with the children on his back. You might be
with him and taking it all in and then a little later, long after
you've read the books, you realize, 'I've met the same character in
the real world, where we call him Jesus.'

"Just for a little while, while you're reading the Narnia stories,
you get your mind off of all the stained glass and Sunday school
associations and various prejudices about the Christian faith, and
you actually attend to someone like Jesus," continued Hooper.
"And your heart is wrung by the goodness of this lion and what
happens and what he says to the children in the book. Then you
come back in the real world from Narnia and see how you had
misrepresented or misunderstood Jesus before. It's so nice to forget churches and all of that and go into Narnia and meet the lion,
Aslan, Jesus as a lion, and to get to know him. No prejudices."

"Lewis saw life in epic proportions," said Mitchell. "He knew that we are engaged in something much bigger than ourselves. The issues are real and the people are real and the world we live in was created by a personal God who was incredibly creative. In Lewis's fiction, he already has your imagination, he has you engaged, but in the process, he can marshal arguments to bear. For example, in *The Silver Chair*, two children are seeking to deliver a prince from being imprisoned by a witch of the underground. In an encounter between the children and the witch, they say they want to go back to Narnia—they don't want to stay in the underground. And the witch begins to say, 'Describe to me this Narnia.' And they describe a sun and all these things and she says, 'Oh, you mean like this light I have here.' And she basically begins to say that everything you think of as Narnia is a projection of the reality that's here. Which is in some ways a Freudian argument in the sense that God is just a projection of ourselves. And Lewis embodies it in this fictional story.

"Lewis's ability to combine these two things was a rare art," continued Mitchell, "He engaged the mind and the imagination together. Very few theological writers are able to do that. I think the other skill that he had is that he tied in to very ancient understandings of human nature—starting back to the Socratic period and Plato and the conception of the human person. I think he appealed to those things. I think he appealed to our sense of right and wrong. Now, we may not accept the Christian conception of right and wrong, but he could bring it over into this parallel world. Tolkien did the same thing. Tolkien said he basically takes this world and he plays it out in this parallel world of Middle

Earth, and we're all on board, and we're all cheering for the right things. And he awakens these things in us. And I think that's what Lewis was doing as well, and he did it intentionally."

The relationship between J. R. R. Tolkien and C. S. Lewis extended beyond their friendship. Some suggest there was a friendly rivalry between them regarding their Christian fictional works. Both The Lord of the Rings and The Chronicles of Narnia series are based in fantasy worlds of myth and magic. Both present epic battles between right and wrong, good and evil. Both are vastly entertaining and enjoyable on the level of pure fun. And both are rooted in their Christian messages and themes. Few would question that Tolkien's The Lord of the Rings and Lewis's The Chronicles of Narnia are both lasting and extremely popular. Still, the books differ widely in their depth, detail, and in their scholarly perception.

Yet the books shared gospel motifs. "The mission in The Lord of the Rings is to restore what had been before in Middle Earth," said Gresham. "But that was also the mission of Jesus Christ, to restore the perfection that God had originally created and that we messed up in the Garden of Eden. And in a sense, that also is the mission in The Chronicles of Narnia: to restore to perfection the 'True Narnia,' once you get through the illusory veil of death that had been created in the first place."

Tolkien and Lewis both shared parts of their work in meetings of the Inklings, where it was evaluated and critiqued by their colleagues. Lewis even read his nearly completed manuscript for *The Lion, the Witch and the Wardrobe* to Tolkien in late December 1948. But Tolkien's response was not what Lewis had hoped for. While Lewis said that he loved The Lord of the Rings, the opposite was true of Tolkien's feelings toward The Chronicles of Narnia.

"They didn't always agree in terms of the rules behind what you do," said Mitchell. "Tolkien didn't like The Chronicles of Narnia, and that was because Tolkien was a purist and Lewis would mix certain fantasy elements together in a way that Tolkien would never think of doing. For example, he brought Father Christmas into this parallel world called Narnia. Tolkien believed Father Christmas had no business being in Narnia. But Lewis loved The Lord of the Rings. And they did encourage one another."

"Jack took a more eclectic view and mixed a lot of things together," said Gresham. "Tolkien's Middle Earth mythology is very pure; Jack's Narnia mythology is very mixed. So the relationship between the books is somewhat antipathetic. On the one hand we have crystal-clear, pure mythology from Tolkien—some of the greatest Christian literature that has ever been written. It's beautiful stuff. In a sense, the whole of The Lord of the Rings is one great poem. On the other hand, you have the Narnia chronicles, which are a mixture of all kinds of mythology and mythological thinking—all the ideas and thoughts of man searching for God brought together and presented in a heap, together with God's reaching out to man—all in one series of books. So they're at opposite ends of the scale in the genre."

"I think Lewis and Tolkien were effectively in competition," said Manlove. "But I think it was rather more often from Tolkien's side. Certainly when he read *The Lion, the Witch and the Wardrobe* he thought it was awful stuff. But they're very different writers, and Tolkien may have realized how different they were. Lewis was not fundamentally concerned with the past in the way Tolkien was. Tolkien's books are all elegies and, at least certainly in The Lord of the Rings, he was always looking backward."

"And yet there was a commonality between them, which was a shared depth of understanding of language," added Gresham. "It's rather like the books themselves are beautiful pieces of architecture. If you build an arch, a Gothic arch for example, every stone is an essential, key part and without each part, the arch simply won't work. Both The Lord of the Rings and The Chronicles of Narnia are built that way. Every word has its place in the book, and to be perfect every word must be there. That's why it's so difficult to abbreviate either of those two works. If you picked up, a thousand years hence, a copy of *The Lion, the Witch and the Wardrobe* and read it, and then picked up a copy of *The Hobbit* [the prequel to The Lord of the Rings trilogy] and read it, you would know that the two men, Tolkien and Lewis, probably knew each other, probably grew up in the same time under similar circumstances and in similar societies. They probably went to the same university and probably studied similar subjects."

As popular as The Chronicles of Narnia are as a series, *The Lion, the Witch and the Wardrobe* has enjoyed a life of its own. The book has been illustrated for calendars and performed as a stage play. After more than fifty years in print, it remains uniquely popular among children around the world.

"It's very popular among children because it tells a good story," said Manlove. "It did this by means of suspense and drawing you in. One of the ways Lewis did this was through the tactile. The perfect example is of Lucy (the youngest of the four siblings) getting into the wardrobe and feeling her way through the fur coats— gradually going through and keeping her hands out before her because she doesn't want to hit the back of the wardrobe. And then she reaches farther and touches what looks like prickly stuff. There's a crunch under her feet and she thinks it's a lot of mothballs, but when she bends down to touch them, she feels that they're cold. And suddenly she's in the middle of a snowfall in the wood.

"It's that process of actually tapering the ordinary into the extraordinary and the unknown that draws you in," continued Manlove. "And Lewis used it again and again in his books. He started with the perfectly ordinary, a railway station, a girl crying behind a gym at school, two kids who are reluctant guests of a brat called Eustace in *The Voyage of the Dawn Treader*, and so on. And then he suddenly transports you into Narnia."

It can also be argued that the characters in Narnia have a universal, archetypal nature of their own that draws readers into the adventure.

"Lucy, Edmund, Peter, and Susan are evacuees from a country besieged by war. They're four children who come to stay with their uncle and who find their way into Narnia. There has long been a prophecy in Narnia that there will be two sons of Adam and two daughters of Eve who will sit on the thrones of Cair Paravel and become the kings and queens of Narnia. Aslan's appearance has long been predicted, too, and these two predictions came together in Narnia. I think they are archetypes in the sense that it's the anima-animus together, two of them. And the 'four' is Jung's idea of wholeness. They come together on the thrones of Cair Paravel as a unification of perfection—a kind of perfection brought together.

"The children can be seen as parts of the soul," continued Manlove, "not as essential parts of the soul but as different aspects of human behavior. Lucy is the imagination; she's always the one who sees first. She sees Aslan in a way the others don't. She's got an inward sight, a spiritual vision. Peter is the steady, rational one. He's very strong and courageous. Edmund is the weaker side, the side that's much more skeptical. I think he's representative of what Lewis abhorred in modern culture—the questioning of obvious value. For example, when Lucy's been to Narnia and he's been to Narnia, he pretends he hasn't been there. He's prepared to lie about the truth in order to serve his own purposes and to be the top dog. Susan? I think she's the appetites in many ways. She often says, 'I'm hungry.' And in fact, significantly, she's removed from the last Narnia book, having gotten too old.

"But the big question is, What does Aslan represent in man?" continued Manlove. "Or beyond man? I think he's God in man, the God that is incarnate in some sense, or incarnate in his creation. He visits us and he's at the bottom of it. There's a chap named George Macdonald, whom Lewis owed a lot to, and he used to believe that God lived inside of your unconscious, in your imagination. He actually had this sort of little cell in there and he would send up all sorts of messages to your mind from that innermost cave. While Lewis would not have gone that far, I think he probably felt that the inward prompting of goodness in the characters was very much Aslan at work.

"[Lewis] always stated that the evangelical and transformative purpose of his books was not the first one. That is, he wrote and expressed what he was best able to do, then expected that would have its own moral effect without his looking for it. I think he almost assigned it to Aslan."

—COLIN MANLOVE

"The witch, at first, seemed a fairy-tale witch who wanted the children to do naughty things. She gave them sweet things to drink and Turkish Delight to bribe them. And then her evil became much more profound. She became associated with the most hideous horrors. She wanted to destroy all life around her until there was nothing at all. So is she evil? Yes. Though I don't know if you could say she's Satan. But she is that principle, that tendency toward nonentity."

As for the wardrobe itself? According to Manlove, "The wardrobe is a symbol of enclosure and the children coming out of it into a new country is, in a sense, a way of going into the soul. I think the land, Narnia, is the landscape of the spirit. It is certainly a way of going out of the self. Not that everyone who goes into Narnia is unselfish: witness Edmund. But even Edmund's actions are a prelude to his self-betterment via Aslan's help."

Throughout The Chronicles of Narnia there is a sense of majesty and grandeur. Lewis had a way of showing us that what we take for granted in our world is actually quite extraordinary.

"Lewis was a great democrat, make no mistake," noted Manlove. "That's why the children become kings and queens of Narnia. He had a sense of ceremony and hierarchy as being part of the everlasting nature of the world. Everyone finds oneself in one's proper place, even though one may meet across them. So that's part of it; he wrote hierarchically in style because that was the cast of his mind. He also had an acute sensitivity to language because of his great sense of the particular. His power in imagery came from his peculiar grasp of the real world. He had a very, very strong sense of the outer world, which translated into a very, very strong sense of every little datum that can be used to alter the mind.

"With Lewis, I always know that he knows more than I do," continued Manlove. "I think a lot of people have felt this, that they're missing out. Not from an inquisitive point of view, more as if they're failing themselves. The mind that made all these fantastic worlds, all of Narnia, that mind was incredibly rich. And it was given that richness by virtue of his faith. There's no denying it. It's not just Lewis's imagination, it's his faith. You're permitted, as you're reading the books, to enjoy reading them and to enter these places and experience them, as removed as you are. But you can never enjoy them as Lewis did. I always feel he's nearer to the center of things than I will ever be."

As a defining characteristic of many great fictional works, people often question whether a book will continue to enjoy sales and develop new readers well into the future. Thus far, both Tolkien and Lewis seem to have created lasting works in the fantasy genre, each with annual sales in the millions. Since its original publication, it's estimated that The Lord of the Rings trilogy has sold more than fifty million copies and has been translated into twenty-six languages. And sales of The Chronicles of Narnia are soaring.

"Will The Chronicles of Narnia be eternal?" mused Gresham. "As long as literature lasts, they will last. And I think the reason is because they're true. The works of Dickens show the truth about society as it was at that time, and so on. All the greatest literature we have is based on truth, based on the eternal truth of the war between good and evil. One of the greatest fictional pieces written for adults in current times is *The Lord of the Rings*. It's one of the most powerful Christian books ever written, because it contains the essential truth."

"I don't think Lewis would have cared himself," said Manlove. "I'm not sure Tolkien would have either. They would have said their works were written piously enough for the greater glorification of God. I mean Tolkien actually does say this at the end of *Tree & Leaf*. He says, 'We create in the image of the Creator, and we don't know what form our works may come true in. They may go beyond the walls of this world, but it's not for us to say.' With Lewis, nothing is permanent. Narnia is destroyed. In his book *Out of the Silent Planet*, Malacandra is a ruined world. So Lewis was acutely aware of flux and he was indifferent to it. I feel if he'd have awakened now and looked at *The Lion, the Witch and the Wardrobe* being fifty years old, he would have laughed. I think he would have been very happy, no doubt, but there's that side of him that wouldn't have cared at all."

CHAPTER EIGHT

A CHANGE OF HEART

*A*fter a stay of several months in an Oxford nursing home, Mrs. Moore died of influenza on January 12, 1951. She was buried in the graveyard at Holy Trinity Church in Headington Quarry. Warnie, who was far from admiring of Mrs. Moore, did not attend the funeral. And after her prolonged illness and coping with her failing mental faculties, even C. S. Lewis might have considered her death a relief.

"She was suffering from dementia," said Dorsett. "She went into a nursing home and he visited her almost daily. Her death wasn't tragic. She wasn't young. She wasn't well. It was a great relief."

"Before her death it had become very difficult," said Mitchell.

"Like all of us, when we see death occur for someone who's very ill, we feel both a sense of regret and relief."

———— • ————

With success come new challenges and C. S. Lewis was, by the early 1950s, besieged with correspondence.

"His burden of correspondence was huge," said Gresham, "and that was what he found to be the chief result of fame. Everyone seems to want to become rich and famous. Yet when you experience that, as Jack did, it becomes an enormous burden. I think Jack's commitment to his correspondence was largely a matter of compassion, a matter of his interest in other people."

"Some people are set apart to care for souls," added Dorsett. "Lewis had a keen sense of that. He never could have made it as a parish priest because he didn't have the ability to sit down and talk to people one-on-one. But he could do it through the mail. He could help people wrestle with their problems. He took the letters very seriously and he gave people the attention they couldn't find in other places."

Despite the burden it placed on his time, it was through his correspondence that Lewis began an encounter that not only changed his life, it crystallized his emotional and spiritual core.

Enter Joy Davidman Gresham. Born in New York City in 1915, Joy was gifted with an exceptional intellect. After undergraduate studies at New York's Hunter College, she completed her master's degree in English literature at Columbia University by the time

JOY DAVIDMAN LEWIS.

she was twenty. Soon after, Joy joined the Communist Party, and, during that time, she won the 1938 Yale Younger Poets Award for her book of poetry called *Letter to a Comrade*. In 1940, she published a novel entitled *Anya*.

During a Communist Party meeting in 1942, Joy met a writer named William Gresham. They were married and had two children: David (born in 1944) and Douglas (born in 1945). What's been written previously and discussions with both Hooper and Dorsett suggest that Joy and Bill had a tumultuous marriage and that Bill suffered problems related to alcohol and depression.

By the late 1940s, marital problems and her own inquisitive mind had pushed Joy into a spiritual journey. Like Lewis, she moved from atheism to a belief in Christianity. For Joy, Lewis's writings played a significant role in her conversion.

According to Lyle Dorsett, who wrote *And God Came In: A Biography of Joy Davidman*, "Joy, like many people who lived in the twentieth century, was searching for something. And in her search, she encountered the writings of C. S. Lewis. Lewis's writings led her to the New Testament. The New Testament pointed her to Jesus Christ and she became a Christian. She was so influenced by Lewis that she wanted to engage him in some question-and-answer.

"She went up to Vermont and talked with Chad Walsh, the author of the first Lewis biography entitled *C. S. Lewis: Apostle to the Skeptics*. She went with Bill Gresham, with her two boys, just to ask Walsh questions about Lewis. 'What would Lewis think about this?' 'What would Lewis say about that?' And Walsh said, 'Why don't you write to Lewis?'"

It's believed that Joy's first letter to Lewis arrived in January 1950 and, like most of his correspondence at the time, it was probably opened by Warnie. The letter was apparently striking enough in substance that Warnie singled it out. After reading it, Lewis wrote back.

"He really enjoyed the correspondence," said Hooper. "He had a lot of letters to write, but these he really did enjoy. I mean, he didn't just enjoy writing to her. He enjoyed her letters."

"My mother's correspondence with Jack started off as just another fan writing," said Joy's son Douglas Gresham. "But of course, because of her education and her intellectual abilities, her letters were different. Her letters were revealments of this amazingly powerful mind. She was somewhat immature when she began to write to him, certainly, but she had a mind seeking truth, which was something Jack deeply respected—the search for truth."

"At the time she was growing up it became evident to her that you either became a Nazi and conquered the world or you became a Communist and saved it," continued Gresham. "She searched for that kind of philosophical truth. She tried Communism, found it utterly lacking, dropped it, and continued to search for truth. She was always looking for truth in her young life. It was the whole mark of my mother's personality. And so having written to Jack and having established this pen-friendship, this correspondence back and forth across the Atlantic Ocean, she was determined to try to meet the man. And she did, in fact, in 1952, and they became friends."

At the time of their first meeting, Joy visited Lewis as part of a longer trip she'd planned to London. She left the boys in America with Bill and under the care of a cousin named Renee Pierce. Lewis was apparently intrigued by Joy's intellect, and Joy was certainly aware of Lewis's stature even as she sought his guidance and spiritual counsel. On the afternoon of September 24, 1952, Lewis and Warnie met Joy Gresham for afternoon tea. The rendezvous occurred in the restaurant at the Eastgate Hotel across the street from Magdalen College. For Joy, the meeting was the culmination of a long journey of self-discovery—but she wasn't intimidated.

"Lewis was a towering figure," said Dorsett. "But he didn't try to overwhelm people. He wasn't prideful in that way, but people were often frightened of him. Joy wasn't. They had a sort of intellectual tennis match. And she could knock the ball back across the court to him just as fast as he could to her, and he loved it. But he also was attracted to her just as a woman, as a friend."

While Joy was still visiting England, she received a letter from her husband indicating that he'd become involved with her cousin, Renee. She returned to the United States and eventually divorced her husband. Then, despite financial difficulties, she and her two sons moved to London.

"When my mother and my father finally split up completely, my mother fled from America to England where, at that time, it was cheaper to live," said Gresham, "and where she thought she

> "Some people are set apart to care for souls. Lewis had a keen sense of that. He never could have made it as a parish priest because he didn't have the ability to sit down and talk to people one-on-one. But he could do it through the mail. He could help people wrestle with their problems. He took the letters very seriously and he gave people the attention they couldn't find in other places."
>
> —LYLE DORSETT

could find a better education for her children. She was struggling financially and Jack's charity came to the fore. He helped her

> "My mother's correspondence
> with Jack started off as just another fan
> writing. But of course, because of her
> education and her intellectual abilities,
> her letters were different. Her letters
> were revealments of this amazingly
> powerful mind. She was somewhat
> immature when she began to write to
> him, certainly, but she had a mind seeking
> truth, which was something Jack deeply
> respected—the search for truth."
>
> —DOUGLAS GRESHAM

through a lot of difficult times, and I think that was the beginning of their emotional relationship."

Joy settled at first in London and sent her sons to school in Surrey. Her divorce from Bill Gresham was finalized in 1954. No one knows for sure whether Lewis assisted her with expenses; however, both Doug Gresham and biographer George Sayer believe he did. Though they did visit each other occasionally and their friendship flourished, Joy and Lewis did not spend a lot of time together between her arrival in 1953 and her move to Oxford in 1955.

Still, there were other changes taking shape in Lewis's life that had nothing to do with Joy.

———— • ————

Through most of his adult life, C. S. Lewis was defined by his writing, his teaching, and his friendships with Warnie, Tolkien, and the Inklings. Yet despite his lengthy and acclaimed tenure at Oxford, he was repeatedly denied a professorship and role as head of the department.

"Lewis was never offered a chair at Oxford, and some think it was because of his overt Christian faith and the time he spent writing in that arena," said Mitchell. "It's possible they thought that he would not have the time to put toward the kinds of academic writings the professorship would require. It seems to me that assumption is somewhat lame, in that he continued to put out scholarly works throughout, probably more than most Oxford dons, while keeping up this other field of writing. It's been suggested there were jealousies in terms of his popularity. I mean, Oxford dons do not get their picture on *Time* magazine; Lewis did."

Dorsett added, "The truth is, Lewis was a first-rate scholar. Like the volume he wrote in The Oxford History of English Literature series called *English Literature in the 16th Century, Excluding Drama* (retitled *Poetry and Prose in the 16th Century* when republished in 1990)—it is still the standard work on the sixteenth century in English literature. A number of his academic works are still standard. But he didn't get the professorship. I think part of it was jealousy; part of it, though, was that there were people who thought Lewis was too up-front with his Christian faith."

Even Lewis's longtime friends J. R. R. Tolkien and Owen Barfield suggested that Lewis might have become too overt in his evangelism. "I think it's wrong to make the assumption that Lewis was obviously the best person for each of the positions that were open," said Mitchell. "Maybe that wasn't the case. But from what I've been able to read and understand, his popularity on a lay level, his willingness to write outside the academic community, to write for the common person, and especially to write theology and Christianity, were part of the problem. I think that all worked against him."

His overt faith? Jealousy of his popular success? Perhaps. No one knows for sure. But for Lewis, being denied a professorship by his alma mater was a painful sidebar to an otherwise illustrious career. Everything changed, however, in January 1955. After more than thirty years at Oxford University, Lewis accepted the professorship of medieval and Renaissance literature at Magdalen College in Cambridge. Lewis had friends and admirers at Cambridge and his appointment was made with an unanimous vote of the electing committee.

Though Lewis was known to find the process of change to be a challenge, his friends at Oxford, including Tolkien, convinced him to take the job. "There's a wonderful letter from Tolkien to Lewis," said Mitchell. "It encouraged him to accept the professorship at Cambridge and gave him reasons why he should do it. And he convinced Lewis."

From 1955 through 1962, Lewis split his time between the two cities. He used the train to commute between his weekly academic life in Cambridge and the weekends and holidays he continued to enjoy at the Kilns in Oxford.

Cambridge is a very different town from Oxford. It's smaller and lacks the industrial base that makes Oxford a blend of past and present. Still, Cambridge University rivals Oxford in both reputation and beauty. Though Lewis may have been somewhat unnerved by the move, it was certainly a step forward in his career. And over time, he grew to like Cambridge a great deal. It's also interesting to note that upon Lewis's departure, Magdalen College, Oxford, chose to elect him to an honorary fellowship.

CHAPTER NINE

LOVE

*I*n late 1955, after Joy Gresham and her sons, David and Douglas, had relocated to Old High Street in Headington near Oxford, the British government refused her permission to continue to live and work in England.

Lyle Dorsett believes the British authorities perceived Joy as a liability. "It's the 1950s. Why couldn't this American stay?" questioned Dorsett. "Well, first of all, she had no real means of support. She wasn't married and she's a writer that makes hardly any money. There's no child support coming in. Another problem is that she had been involved with the Communist Party in the United States in the thirties and there was a lot of Communist-scare stuff going on in Britain in the 1950s. So the government could have thought, *We really don't need this woman here.* Jack felt this was horrid, so he did all he could to make sure that she wouldn't be deported."

"Jack married her in a civil ceremony so that she wouldn't have to go back," said Dorsett. "He was concerned, and he didn't want the boys to be back there with their father, who was a bit violent at times when he was drinking. But Joy and Jack did not consummate the marriage because Lewis did not believe it was a real marriage. It was just a matter of convenience. He didn't want her to leave the country."

By creating a legal marriage, Lewis's citizenship was extended to both Joy and her sons. The ceremony occurred on April 23, 1956.

"They got married before they fell in love," said Gresham. "And then they fell in love afterward. And I think the unfolding of this relationship was really based in Jack's charity and friendship. Simply by means of a charitable extension of his citizenship to her, my mother could stay in England and I'm a British citizen."

There's no evidence to suggest that Lewis and Joy were in love at the time of the civil ceremony. Though they were often companions, Lewis and Joy did not (at first) live together. Still, the relationship began to change. Within just months of their legal marriage, Joy began to experience severe pain in the upper part of her left leg. In late October, she fell while alone at home. Once conveyed to the hospital, Joy was diagnosed with terminal cancer.

"I interviewed her physician," said Dorsett, "and he told me,

'I've never seen anybody more eaten up with cancer. Her femur had broken in two, and the bones were filled with cancer. Her thoracic and abdominal cavities were filled with cancer.' And he said, 'I had her in the hospital, and I told Jack, "She's got ten days, maybe two weeks to live."'"

While Joy was hospitalized, Lewis's emotional attachment grew stronger. As a lifelong bachelor, he may not have been accustomed to expressing his affection. Or perhaps he was finally able to appreciate just how deep his affection for Joy really was.

"I suppose the loss of this woman stimulated Jack to finally admit to himself and realize that he was in love with her," said Gresham. "Because of his lack of experience, I don't think he really knew what was happening to him emotionally. He realized, I think, that he had fallen in love with her and decided to marry her on her deathbed. Which he did."

Regardless of how he was able to define it, Lewis made the decision that he wanted to marry Joy in a Christian ceremony. The problem was, Lewis's bishop wouldn't allow it because Joy was divorced. At the same time, though, Lewis invited an Anglican priest named Peter Bide to visit Joy in the hospital. Bide was reputed to be a healer.

"When Bide would pray for people, often there were physical healings," said Dorsett. "Lewis invited him up to Oxford to pray for Joy's healing, which he did. He came up and spent the night. While they're talking, and this is what Bide told me, Jack said to him, 'You know the one thing I wish Joy could have? Her dying wish is that our marriage could be recognized by the church. She'd love to be married in the church.' And Bide said, 'We're not going to deny this woman her dying wish.' Lewis countered, 'But the bishop won't allow it.' Bide responded, 'He's not my bishop; I will perform the wedding.' So the next morning, in the hospital, with the nurse and Warnie as attendants, Father Bide consecrated the marriage.

"But he also prayed for her healing," added Dorsett. "And a few days later, she walked out of the hospital. Some can write it off as just typical remission, but according to her physician, she was way past that."

> "He realized, I think, that he had fallen in love with [Joy] and decided to marry her on her deathbed. Which he did."
>
> —DOUGLAS GRESHAM

Joy and her sons moved into the Kilns, and Lewis became both her caretaker and her husband as well as a stepfather to the boys. And somewhere during the time between their civil ceremony and Joy's move into the Kilns, Joy and Jack had fallen in love.

"There was one moment in their experience together when

my mother realized that she had fallen head over heels in love with him," said Gresham. "And I think it took place while he was being attentive and taking care of her as a sort of auxiliary nurse at that stage. She had been sent home to die at the Kilns. She was thought, at that time, likely to live only a few days, maybe a matter of hours. I think he'd already fallen and realized his love for her when she was in the hospital, before she went home to die."

"Many people want to protect Lewis by saying, 'He really didn't love her. She maneuvered him. He wouldn't have loved a divorced woman,'" said Dorsett. "I've heard people, at various times, say, 'Lewis married that New York Jew.' I find it shocking, the anti-Semitism I encounter. But I think Lewis fell in love with her very early. I think he was attracted to her mind.

"Chad Walsh told me that she was in love with Lewis before she ever met him," continued Dorsett. "Let's face it, she might have been infatuated, but love? There's no way she could have been in love with him if she hadn't met him. Not really. Because love grows from sharing sufferings and joys and washing one another's feet. Their love grew in that environment."

According to Walter Hooper, "When he married Joy ecclesiastically in the hospital in 1957 and took her home, it's then that romantic love took over. I know everybody wants it to start with *eros,* and they don't care how it ends as long as it starts with *eros,* but it just plain didn't. And Lewis, in writing to one of his old pupils, said, 'It started with pity.' And then after pity came affection, just from knowing her. And after that came the other big love, friendship. And then charity when he married her. And finally, last of all, came *eros.*"

Just as no one knows exactly when Joy and Jack fell in love, it can also be argued that no one knows with certainty the details of their sex life. Some believe it's of little consequence or significance. Still, roughly fifty years after their second, spiritual marriage, discussion continues over whether Lewis and Joy actually consummated their marriage.

"I would have never even raised the question when I was writing the biography [*And God Came In*] if it hadn't been that others raised the question," said Dorsett. "When people get married, you assume they consummate the marriage. Nobody needs to poke into the details. But Walter Hooper made it an issue. And once he made it an issue, it had to be dealt with. And when you read a book like *The Inklings* and you see this strange little note on the bottom of the page: 'There is no evidence this marriage was consummated'—my goodness."

Though clearly exasperated by the controversy, Dorsett continued, "We don't know with certainty. There are no children, and even if there were children, we wouldn't know with certainty without DNA testing. But how do we know there wasn't a sexual relationship—on what grounds? Walter says that she was just way too sick. That's just not so. George Sayer knew Jack, and he said it's absurd to think that this wasn't a normal marriage. Is he without any discernment? Is he a liar? I think not. And there's plenty of evidence that Jack had a robust sexuality before he met Joy. I mean, he wasn't a philanderer. He became a Christian. I don't think he had any affairs after he became a Christian. But he certainly had been around women and that's apparent in the things he's written. Joy and Jack were healthy people and they were married."

"For me it's not an issue," said Mitchell. "My perspective is that they waited until they got married and, again, it's just not that interesting."

Gresham, who lived at the Kilns with his mother and Lewis, supports Dorsett in his conclusion. He states with certainty that Lewis and his mother consummated their marriage. And he also agrees with Mitchell that it's just not that interesting.

While a few scholars and biographers continue to debate the issue, many (including this writer) believe the discussion is ultimately a waste of time. While it's relevant to recognize the profile of the discussion, it is, frankly, a matter that can't be resolved. Perhaps it's time to put it to rest with the simple question: *Who cares?*

What is known for certain is far more telling. Lewis was rarely far from Joy's side during the four years before her death. They enjoyed a close, dynamic, and intellectual companionship.

"For fun, Jack and my mother did things like walk in the woods," said Gresham. "They played word games with each other. They had their own rather unique rules for Scrabble. They would take one board and both sets of letters from two Scrabble sets. And then they would proceed to play Scrabble, allowing all known languages, whether factual or fictional, and they would fill the whole board with words.

"They also read poetry to each other. They read what they

C. S. AND JOY AT THE KILNS.

regarded as really good prose to each other. They spent a lot of time in conversation. And they spent a lot of time in silence, each reading their own books. It was companionable silence.

"I think what she gained mainly from their relationship," continued Gresham, "was a sense of security, a sense of peace that she could now actually die. She was secure in the knowledge that there was someone to look after her sons. I also think the experience of living with and loving Jack enriched their Christianity a great deal and deepened their understanding of Christ. It's completely conjectural, whether she was ever fully committed to Christ until quite close to the end of her life. But I think it would have been Jack's influence that brought her to the final stage of that commitment. I have no evidence, of course. Certainly, she had a sense of security and safety which she had never experienced in her life before, and a great deal of happiness—enormous happiness. That period between her remission and the reemergence of her cancer was the happiest time of her life. And of his, I think, too."

After Joy's cancer went into remission, they took several holidays together. Joy worked on redecorating the Kilns and she helped Lewis with his writing, including *The Four Loves,* which was published in 1960. They enjoyed an active social life and the two boys, who were attending boarding schools, spent their holidays at the Kilns as well. Lewis's writings during this time, especially his letters, were filled with references to his profound love for Joy. It can be stated with relative certainty that their love grew throughout their marriage and that it became a special relationship anchored by their faith.

Then, during the spring of 1960, Joy's cancer returned. Perhaps with the knowledge that this might be her last chance, she and Lewis took a long-anticipated trip to Greece. Along with friends, they visited many of the classic Greek ruins, including Delphi, Mycenae, and the Acropolis. For Joy, it was a dream fulfilled. For Lewis, it was a rare chance to see the places he'd read about for more than fifty years.

"They had a very good time," said Hooper. "It was simply the perfect ending to Joy's life in a way. She was able to climb up the Acropolis and see the Parthenon. And Lewis said, 'Even though she knew she was dying, and even though she knew that I knew she was dying, when we heard those shepherds playing their flutes in the hills of Greece, it just didn't make any difference.' Joy was losing her life, but she had married the man she loved and nobody, nobody could shake her out of that happiness."

Though fulfilling on many levels, the trip to Greece left Joy physically exhausted. After her return, her need for care became constant. She was admitted to the Acland Nursing Home on June 20 but still managed a final recovery a few days later, and she returned to the Kilns on June 27. Her final days included long hours with Lewis and even a country drive in the Cotswolds. On

"For fun, Jack and my mother did
things like walk in the woods. They played
word games with each other. They had
their own rather unique rules for Scrabble.
They would take one board and both
sets of letters from two Scrabble sets.
And then they would proceed to play
Scrabble, allowing all known languages,
whether factual or fictional, and they would
fill the whole board with words."

—DOUGLAS GRESHAM

July 13, Joy's condition became suddenly worse. She was rushed to the hospital and, at approximately 10:15 that night, Joy Davidman Gresham Lewis died.

Four days after her death, Joy's body was cremated. C. S. Lewis, Warnie, Douglas, David, and several family friends were in attendance as her ashes were scattered at the Headington Crematorium. A nearby marble plaque bears the following poignant inscription:

Remember

Helen Joy

Davidman

D. July 1960

Loved wife of C. S. Lewis

And beneath it is an epitaph based on one of Lewis's poems that reads:

Here the whole world (stars, water, air,

And field, and forest, as they were

Reflected in a single mind)

Like cast off clothes was left behind

In ashes yet with hope that she,

Re-born from holy poverty,

In lenten lands, hereafter may

Resume them on her Easter Day.[1]

CHAPTER TEN

A GRIEF OBSERVED

$\mathcal{L}$ove came to C. S. Lewis late in his life, but when it arrived, it arrived with a strength and passion that many long for and few achieve. The love between C. S. Lewis and Joy Davidman Gresham has been well documented in books such as Lyle Dorsett's *And God Came In* and Douglas Gresham's *Lenten Lands*. It was immortalized in two film adaptations: the BBC television production of *Shadowlands* featuring Claire Bloom as Joy and Joss Ackland as C. S. Lewis, and the Richard Attenborough production of *Shadowlands* featuring Debra Winger as Joy and Anthony Hopkins as C. S. Lewis.

While both films captured the love story in great detail, they

AT THE KILNS WITH DAVID AND DOUGLAS GRESHAM, 1957.

paid little attention to Lewis's life after Joy's death. During the first year, Lewis did what he could to maintain his routine while dealing with new physical challenges of his own. He was suffering from infected kidneys. Yet he still met regularly with the Inklings and continued his work at Cambridge. In 1961, he published a scholarly work called *An Experiment in Criticism*.

But Lewis was also coping with a deep and challenging sense of loss. He began work on what would become one of his most highly regarded books, *A Grief Observed*.

"It's a tiny little book," said Gresham, "but it's a completely honest look at grief and what it was doing to him. And for a while there, his faith in God—not his faith in the existence of God, but his faith in the nature of God—was sorely tested. He was driven to the very brink of believing that God was a sadistic, murdering swine of a character. And then, once the pain started to recede, he was able to see that it was pain driving his thinking rather than his thinking controlling the pain.

"The pain itself had enormous value," continued Gresham, "because it's only by the pain of bereavement that we can gauge the degree and the depth of our love for the person who's gone.

It's the only yardstick we have to measure how much we love someone. I think *A Grief Observed* reveals all of this. It allows us to look at grief honestly, and to relate to the book based on what's happening to Jack and what's happening to us at the same time."

"*A Grief Observed* really is a work on the power of grief," said Mitchell. "Lewis was able to order his life quite well. What grief did was just create havoc. He couldn't control the grief, and that was extremely unsettling for him. The writing out of it was his way of trying to articulate what was going on inside. What he realized is that grief is not a state, it's more like a history. It has an ongoing life and there are phases in that grief. He wanted to say, 'Okay, what is this? What's going on with me? This is something very, very new.' And he called it 'passionate grief.' It's a grief that grips you and controls you."

Mitchell continued, "Here was probably the most intimate relationship of his life coming to an end, and now he's processing it as a Christian. What his grief did was make him want to hit back—to strike out. And what became the object of his striking out? His faith. Grief robbed him of his understanding of joy, and his love for Joy and God. Passionate grief brought everything into doubt. It authenticated and validated the problem of pain."

Early in chapter 3 of *A Grief Observed,* Lewis wrote:

> Feelings, and feelings, and feelings. Let me try thinking instead. From the rational point of view, what new factor has H's death introduced into the problem of the universe? What grounds has it given me for doubting all that I believe? I knew already that these

things, and worse, happened daily. I would have said that I had taken them into account. I had been warned—I had warned myself—not to reckon on worldly happiness. We were even promised sufferings. They were part of the programme. We were even told, "Blessed are they that mourn" and I accepted it. I've got nothing that I hadn't bargained for. Of course it is different when the thing happens to oneself, not to others, and in reality, not in imagination. Yes; but should it, for a sane man, make quite such a difference as this? No. And it wouldn't for a man whose faith had been real faith and whose concern for other people's sorrows had been real concern. The case is too plain. If my house has collapsed at one blow, that is because it was a house of cards. The faith which "took these things into account" was not faith but imagination. The taking them into account was not real sympathy. If I had really cared, as I thought I did, about the sorrows of the world, I should not have been so overwhelmed when my own sorrow came. It has been an imaginary faith playing with innocuous counters labeled "Illness," "Pain," "Death," and "Loneliness." I thought I trusted the rope until it mattered to me whether it would bear me. Now it matters, and I find I didn't.[1]

Despite the challenges Lewis made to his own faith, he discovered, during the course of grieving, a renewed sense of faith and the healing that comes with it.

"Lewis used the example of a man whose leg has been amputated," said Mitchell. "That man will live with that loss forever. But does it debilitate him all of his life? Well, it depends on how

"[*A Grief Observed*] is a tiny
little book, but it's a completely honest
look at grief and what it was doing
to him. And for a while there, his faith
in God—not his faith in the existence of
God, but his faith in the nature of God—
was sorely tested. He was driven to the
very brink of believing that God was
a sadistic, murdering swine of a character.
And then, once the pain started to recede,
he was able to see that it was pain driving
his thinking rather than his thinking
controlling the pain."

—Douglas Gresham

one responds, but for the most part, no. He gets over that debil-
itating part, but he never gets over the fact that he's lost a leg. It's
always with him. So in this history of grief, there are levels of
healing."

"He trusted God because he knew his character," noted

Dorsett. "And Lewis could say in *A Grief Observed,* 'Sometimes my prayer life is like pounding on a door that's bolted shut from the other side.' He didn't doubt that God was on the other side. But he didn't understand why he wasn't hearing anything back at the moment, why the connectedness wasn't there. Faith was absolutely essential."

Lewis wrote in chapter 4:

> I was wrong to say that the stump was recovering from the pain of the amputation. I was deceived because it has so many ways to hurt me that I discover them only one by one.
>
> Still, there are two enormous gains—I know myself too well now to call them "lasting." Turned to God, my mind no longer meets that locked door; turned to H., it no longer meets that vacuum—nor all that fuss about my mental image of her.[2]

A Grief Observed was a very healing book for Lewis to write. According to Douglas Gresham, "He wrote it as his own journal and had no intention of publishing it originally. He wrote it just to keep on paper his own thoughts, his own feelings, in order to analyze what was happening to him. That was what he always turned to in times of stress: pen and ink. It was actually Roger Lancelyn Greene who persuaded him to publish it, when he came down to visit Jack some months after Mother's death. He asked Jack how he was coping and Jack told him he'd written this journal. He used to keep it in the drawer of his desk in his office. And Roger asked if he might read it. And since Roger was a close friend, Jack said yes. Roger then told him, 'Jack, really, you have to publish this. This will help so many people.'"

A Grief Observed was published in 1961; however, Lewis published it under the pseudonym N. W. Clerk. According to Hooper, "He didn't want to draw attention to his own marriage. After all, his marriage was not a very long one, and why should he feel that he was entitled to more respect or more sympathy than other men who'd been married for twenty, thirty, or fifty years?"

"I think it's just that he knew he'd made certain discoveries in marriage and in his grief that he thought would be helpful for people to hear," continued Hooper. "But he didn't want it to be associated with him. He wanted people to think about the argument, but not about C. S. Lewis. And so that's why he used a pseudonym. But later, after Lewis died, we realized the book would reach more people and sell more copies if we put it out under his name, and we replaced the pseudonym."

Once the book was republished under Lewis's name, it became another commercial success. Yet the success was more than financial; *A Grief Observed* offered serious help to those in need of emotional and spiritual healing.

"I found it healing," said Dorsett. "I read it in the wake of a huge personal loss, one that was as senseless as Joy's death. Too young, too painful, why does this happen? And the book spoke to me powerfully. Yes, he suffered. Yes, he was in pain. But he kept on being faithful. And I can listen to a man who did that."

"*A Grief Observed* is, for me, a very painful book to read," said

Gresham. "It's a complete evaluation of what was happening to Jack emotionally, spiritually, and psychologically after the death of my mother. But I do read it. And I also give it to people. I think it's probably the most valuable book ever written to give to someone who is about to be bereaved or has just been bereaved."

In some ways, this was the final chapter in Lewis's writing career as a Christian apologist. What began with *The Problem of Pain* ended, during his lifetime, with *A Grief Observed*. They were two unique yet similar books.

> "Lewis used the example of a man whose leg has been amputated. That man will live with that loss forever. But does it debilitate him all of his life? Well, it depends on how one responds, but for the most part, no. He gets over that debilitating part, but he never gets over the fact that he's lost a leg. It's always with him. So in this history of grief, there are levels of healing."
>
> —CHRISTOPHER W. MITCHELL

"I think one of the big misconceptions people have about *A Grief Observed* is that it is a very different book from *The Problem of Pain*," said Mitchell. "But a close reading of the books shows they're really not that different. In fact, as Lewis climbed out of the difficulty that his grief had created for his intellectual life, he began to reaffirm the very things that he set forth in *The Problem of Pain*. He expressed them differently, and I think he had a deeper understanding of those principles than he had before, but he didn't overthrow those things. Those ideas were the things he fell back on. The temptations he dealt with in *A Grief Observed* were approached or dealt with to some extent in *The Problem of Pain*."

Death was never a stranger to C. S. Lewis. From the childhood loss of his mother, to the war death of his best friend Paddy and the eventual losses of his father and Mrs. Moore, Lewis had learned to process each passing and to move forward. It was only through the loss of Joy that Lewis was forced to turn inward, to test his faith, and to reveal the insights he gained from his grief to readers around the world. Death, he knew, was inevitable. But his faith in God was a choice.

CHAPTER ELEVEN

NOVEMBER 22, 1963

By the middle of 1963, Lewis's health had declined considerably. His kidneys were failing and he had a prostate infection that was spreading throughout his body.

"He was a heavy smoker," said Dorsett. "He drank gallons of tea and I'm sure he didn't eat right. He wasn't well. But in a way, he was probably ready to fold up the tent. He was probably so tired."

"I think there was a measure of sadness that so many things had changed," said Mitchell. "But I also think there was a sense of anticipation. Lewis's faith was as robust as it had ever been. I think he was at peace."

"His death was not something that was unexpected to him,"

"I'm going to tell you what I did next, though some people may not like it. But I think some things that happen on instinct are to be trusted. My first thing to do was to address my prayers to C. S. Lewis. I assumed he was in heaven and I said, 'Please don't forget me.' I just didn't want to lose touch with him. I had absolute certainty that's where he was and I didn't feel ashamed at all about addressing him. It wasn't a conscious choice; I just found myself doing it. Anyway, if God has him where he's not allowed to hear these little letters from us, I think they'll be shown to him later."

—WALTER HOOPER

said Hooper. "He had an infected kidney and an infected prostate gland, both of which could have been operated on and would have been except that the doctors thought his heart was too weak.

In the summer of 1963, he went into a coma while in the hospital and the doctors said he was dying. I was there when he came out of the coma and we were all surprised. Anyway, as he lay there for those two weeks, he wanted me to take a lot of letters but I didn't want to waste the time.

"I became very worried about the fact that he didn't know what had happened to him: that he had almost died, that he had been expected to die. But nobody had mentioned it to him. So I said to him, 'Jack, do you remember in *The Screwtape Letters* where Wormwood says it's far better for human beings to die in rich nursing homes than to go die in wars? If you go off to war, you might get killed. But in a rich nursing home, friends lie. Doctors lie. Nurses lie.' And Jack said, 'I know that better than you do. What are you getting at?' So then I came clean with him and told him what had happened. And he was very interested and he said, 'I'm glad you told me, Walter. What kind of friend would you be, had you not told me?'

"And after that, in the letters I did type for him, he told his friends about how close he had been, how the gates had opened up to eternal life, but that just before he went in, the gates had closed in his face. And he said at one point, 'I'd rather have gone through. But I regard myself as a sentinel on duty. A sentinel stays at his post until his call.'"

Shortly before Lewis fell into a coma, Hooper had begun a relocation from the United States to England. In Warnie's absence, he had been assisting with Lewis's correspondence. But Hooper had to return to the United States in September to teach a final term and to wrap up his own affairs before moving back to Oxford.

Warnie, who had been in Ireland, returned to help Lewis in his final days. His diary recounts the following from November 22, 1963:

> After four o'clock I took him his tea and had a few words with him, finding him thick in his speech, very drowsy, but calm and cheerful. It was the last time we ever spoke to each other.
>
> At five-thirty I heard a crash in his bedroom, and running in, found him lying unconscious at the foot of the bed. He ceased to breathe some three or four minutes after.[1]

"Then came that fateful day," said Hooper. "I was teaching at the University of Kentucky and while coming from a class, I ran into a colleague who told me the unbelievable news that President Kennedy had been shot and might be dying. We heard through the course of the day the terrible news that he did die. When I finally got to my bed that night, a very tired and sad man, I was just about to fall asleep when Douglas Gresham rang me and said, 'I'm so sorry to have to tell you, but Jack died today.' It turns out that he died the same hour that President Kennedy was killed. It was a dreadful day for many of us.

"I'm going to tell you what I did next," continued Hooper, "though some people may not like it. But I think some things that happen on instinct are to be trusted. My first thing to do was to address my prayers to C. S. Lewis. I assumed he was in heaven and I said, 'Please don't forget me.' I just didn't want to lose touch with him. I had absolute certainty that's where he was and I didn't feel ashamed at all about addressing him. It wasn't a conscious choice; I just found myself doing it. Anyway, if God has him where he's not allowed to hear these little letters from us, I think they'll be shown to him later."

LEWIS'S GRAVESTONE IN HEADINGTON QUARRY, OXFORD.

"I didn't realize Jack was dying until it suddenly happened," said Gresham. "I wasn't relieved when Jack died. I hadn't been living in fear of his death. And in a sense, his death left me more bereaved than my mother's death because I didn't expect it. I was eighteen years old in 1963 and I had no parents at all."

With the assassination of President Kennedy leading the news, few people in England or America were able to look beyond to the rest of the day's events. For a man who never really adapted to his celebrity, C. S. Lewis might have smiled knowing that, at the time, few people took note of his death.

Douglas and his brother, David, attended Lewis's funeral four days later at Holy Trinity Church in Headington Quarry. J. R. R. Tolkien, Fred Paxford, and several members of the Inklings were also there. Mrs. Moore's daughter, Maureen, followed the coffin out of the church along with David and Douglas. Apparently because of his intense grief, Warren Lewis, C. S. Lewis's brother and lifelong best friend, did not attend the funeral.

CHAPTER TWELVE

OBSERVATIONS

*T*hroughout the course of doing interviews for both the television documentary and book biography on Lewis, many insights were recorded that did not fit specifically into the narrative. They are, however, some of the most revealing commentary of all and, for that reason, they are presented here as simple observations.

How did C. S. Lewis change your life and work?

"I think he changed my understanding of the way the world is wonderful," said Colin Manlove. "It's quite a surprise to be here at all, but he makes it even more surprising, and he makes you wonder where all of that surprise ultimately comes from. He also appealed to my hunger for the infinite. He makes the infinite incredibly solid. I find very exciting the heaven that he creates in *The Great Divorce*, where there's a stream so solid that the creature from hell can't run about in it, and the waves pierce their feet, or that an apple falls from a tree and goes through them. And there's an enormous solidity about heaven, and an insubstantiality about hell. It moves me. But I can't say that I've become a Christian because of it. He hasn't brought me to commitment."

> "Lewis is saying that if we looked at our own lives, we'd see that they are just as enchanted. A cup of tea here is just as enchanted as a cup of tea in Narnia. A tree here is just as enchanted as a tree in Narnia."
>
> —CHRISTOPHER W. MITCHELL

Did Lewis, in some ways, live in the world of myth and fantasy? Or was he drawing comparisons between this world and his fictional worlds?

"As the director of the Marion E. Wade Center," said Chris Mitchell, "I have been told many times, 'Gosh, I wish I could live in Narnia or I wish I could live in Middle Earth.' When I ask people why, they have all kinds of reasons. Then I ask people, 'Where do you think Lewis or Tolkien got these things, these places?' And they say, 'They got them from right here, earth.' What Lewis and Tolkien did was to take these things and put them into another context where we're not, where we don't bring the same prejudices, where we don't bring the same sort of dulled sensibilities. In those worlds, we open ourselves up in ways that we're not opened to in our daily life here. Lewis gave us new lenses to look at these things.

"From Lewis's perspective," continued Mitchell, "he saw us engaged in a great cosmic warfare, where real issues are at stake with real people, created by a God who created them in this wonderful, incredible way. We have the ability to enjoy so much and yet we have this thing that also corrupts and even works against us. And we're working these things out. But most of us in this world are sort of on the bench. We're not engaged in it. And what Lewis did with his work was to take us off the bench and put us in this other world where we vicariously begin to live more actively. We participate in all these great themes. But the thing is, they all come from our world. And I think that's part of the compelling nature of Lewis's work. All of a sudden, we're reading him and life becomes this exciting thing. Lewis is saying that if we looked at our own lives, we'd see that they are just as enchanted. A cup of tea here is just as enchanted as a cup of tea in Narnia. A tree here is just as enchanted as a tree in Narnia. We're not looking at the world anymore the way we ought to. It really is an enchanted world."

You wrote the book Through the Open Door *about Lewis as part of your graduate work. Can you tell us about your encounter with him?*

"When I arrived in England in 1955, I was assigned to a faculty adviser at King's College University of London who knew Lewis," said Dabney Hart. "In May of that year, my adviser sent the bibliography of my studies on Lewis off to him with a note explaining that I was writing my dissertation on his work. Lewis wrote back, 'If the young lady would care to meet an author who is no very great scholar of his own works, she would be welcome to do so.' And that, of course, was the invitation my adviser and I had been hoping for. He said I could either come to Cambridge during the week or to his home in Oxford on the weekends. I decided it would be more professional to go to Cambridge.

"It was June of 1956, and I recall that it was still rather cool. It was a wonderful welcome. He was about six feet tall, heavyset, with an oval face. It was a very pleasant face, though not striking or distinctive-looking in any way. I'm pretty sure he had on a tweed jacket. He was just the same age as my mother and he gave me the impression that this might be someone whom my father had known in World War I, or some distant cousin from whom I had been separated by an ocean.

"He was so easy to talk to. We talked for some time and he asked what I was doing. And then he said he was going to give me some material to look at and he went into his adjoining study. He gave me a big cardboard box filled with all sorts of things—newspaper clippings, scraps of poems—which I sat and looked at for an hour and a half. Later on, I reflected about this box of material and thought that it must be like the box of toys that a bachelor would keep in the hall closet to bring out for guests who came by with a child—in other words, something to keep a visitor occupied for a while.

"Then he came out to make tea. He had been to a bakery and had bought baked goods for my visit. But he said he wouldn't eat any and apologized because he was 'slimming.' And then we had a lovely, easy conversation. I didn't ask him a single question about his writings because I'd read in an essay that he believed the author says what he wants to say in his work. Then he asked me a question to which the answer was 'No.' He knew I was from the American South and he asked me if I had ever read a novel by Robert Penn Warren called *Band of Angels*. I think he had probably read a lot of American literature, more than he refers to in his criticism, but I hadn't read it. So that was that. End of conversation. Then, when *Till We Have Faces* came out, I realized that he must have read Robert Penn Warren while he was working on the book. And I wondered if Joy had known about it and recommended it to him. So I missed an opportunity there."

Why did you title your book Through the Open Door?

"Lewis made a remark to me at the open door of his rooms at Cambridge that I didn't really understand at the time," said Hart. "As I was leaving, he said to me, 'You'd better hurry up and finish that dissertation before I publish something that might invalidate your conclusions.' Of course, that's the most ominous thing any graduate student can hear, and it was too late to say, 'Oh can't we sit down again and talk about that?'

"I kept turning over in my mind what he'd said and I finally decided that what he meant was that no one knows when he is going to be inspired by grace with some understanding that he didn't have before, some brand-new understanding that may turn his life upside down. And at the time he said it to me I had no idea what he'd been going through in his own personal life during those years. Once I came to the understanding of what he meant, I began to notice in so much of his criticism, in his essays, in his fiction, that he made references to open doors. For example, in a review of one of the volumes of The Lord of the Rings, he said that many critics had tried to identify Tolkien's work as allegory. They all wanted to say that the ring represented Nazism or Communism or technology, or whatever they didn't like. Lewis said they were all wrong. It's not allegory, it's myth. It's a new myth, not an old one, but it's mythic. 'With myth,' he said, 'what you have is a master key. You can use it to open whatever door you want to open.'"

Was the open door symbolic of being open-minded?

"Open-minded, yes, but also open-hearted," continued Hart. "And even more important than being open-minded was keeping an open imagination. In *An Experiment in Criticism,* for example, he justifies his life as a student, critic, and teacher of literature by saying that the importance of teaching literature and reading literature is that it keeps the imagination flexible and open. It nurtures the imagination. And the nurtured imagination is what one needs to be receptive to the operation of grace, whenever it comes and wherever it comes from. So an open mind, that's important; but an open imagination? Even more important."

What can you tell us about C. S. Lewis and prayer?

"I don't think I ever came across a person who prayed so much," said Walter Hooper. "Often in the morning he would get up, go

outside to look at the flowers, and stand right there praying. Then he might come in and read the New Testament in Greek. He could pray anywhere and he could compose himself just like he was writing a book. In a train, on a bus, on a walk, or just standing outside. And he prayed on his knees, too, beside his bed."

"I don't know what he prayed," said Gresham, "but it was not uncommon for me to walk into a room and to find Jack praying. And I would say, 'I'm so sorry, Jack,' and he would say, 'Don't worry, I was only praying.' Prayer for Jack varied enormously. I saw Jack on his knees in prayer. I saw Jack sitting at a desk in prayer. I saw Jack walking in prayer. I could tell if Jack was praying if he was walking around the garden or walking up in the woods or sitting at his desk, but I can't tell you how I could tell. It was just something I knew. He didn't ostentatiously get down on his knees or put his hands together in front of his face and so forth."

As a literary scholar, do you believe the works of both Tolkien and Lewis will last well into the future? Or will they fade?

"I don't think Lewis would have cared himself," said Manlove. "I don't think Tolkien would have either. It's not for us to say. For Tolkien, immortality is something of a threat in the form of the High Elves. It can lead to a certain stupor of the soul. And that's one of the reasons why, possibly, they leave Middle Earth at the end of The Lord of the Rings.

"For Lewis, nothing is permanent. But I do think Lewis speaks to something permanent in our experience. He talks about the infinite. What's always of interest? The infinite. The numinous joy.

That which is perennial in human experience unless we actually close ourselves off to normal human experience. We may do that. It's already questionable whether we actually have the same emotions we did fifty years ago. It's already questionable whether we feel shame in the same way that we did. It's already questionable whether we have the same catalog of manners. So in talking about something six hundred years hence, or six million years hence, the animal that we are as human beings may be radically different. It may find things in Lewis about which we can't even guess. On the other hand, it may find nothing."

What is your favorite C. S. Lewis book, and why?

"I would say that's not a fair question because they are so different from each other," said Hart. "But I'll mention some of my favorites. *An Experiment in Criticism* is one because it's such an original idea—that English literature professors, and that's my profession, should not continue to be the judges of what are great books. Rather, we should say, 'Who are the good readers and what kinds of books do they like to read?' I love that idea.

"I guess another of my favorites is *The Abolition of Man*. And of his major works, *The Great Divorce* is one of my favorites. If you're a Christian seeker, a searcher, then I would recommend *Mere Christianity*. But if you're someone who is fairly well established in the faith and more interested in Lewis's literary works, then I always say, 'Start with *The Great Divorce*.'"

"*Perelandra*," said Manlove. "Most immediately, because of the superb images. They just excite my mind. Like the image of the

"In An Experiment in Criticism . . .
he justifies his life as a student,
critic, and teacher of literature by saying
that the importance of teaching literature
and reading literature is that it keeps the
imagination flexible and open. It nurtures
the imagination. And the nurtured
imagination is what one needs to be
receptive to the operation of grace,
whenever it comes and wherever it
comes from. So an open mind, that's
important; but an open imagination?
Even more important."

—DABNEY HART

ocean that is not an ocean, it's an ocean that's an expression of an angel. Because it's so like something one knows and yet so wholly unlike it. I think Lewis once said, 'When you've got two things so nearly alike, differences are never more apparent.'

"The difference between *Perelandra* and *Out of the Silent Planet* is that in *Out of the Silent Planet,* Lewis is talking about the 'alien.' In *Perelandra,* he's talking about the 'other.' Well, we're talking in mystical terms now, but we're talking about the radically different ontology. And I like it for that reason. I like it because of the very intelligent discussion that goes on about innocence. It penetrates every possible aspect. I think Lewis had thought it out in such a brilliant way. It's not just a boring disposition, it's actually a superb realization. As they talk, the nature of the lady's innocence is being created, and at the same time, so is the man's evil. He's actually building pictures or qualities from discussion. And the gap between discussion and action in *Perelandra* is not real because they are functions of one another and they express one another. The book is so divided between the body and the mind. Lewis's idea in this book is that the body and the mind are intertwined. And he realizes it in the whole structure of the book by having it in a body/mind/body context."

"My favorite C. S. Lewis book," said Mitchell, "depends on what kind of mood I'm in. I've read The Chronicles of Narnia to my children and it's wonderful in terms of an adventure for them. But I think the book that probably moves me most deeply is *Till We Have Faces.* And I think part of the reason is that he comes as close as he ever does to that mythic kind of realm for which he so loved George Macdonald. I also think *The Great Divorce* is not only disturbing, it's great fun. It's hard to pin one down but I would say that one of the best things he ever wrote was his sermon, *The Weight of Glory.* It's probably one of the best things that's found its way into English literature."

"My own favorite," said Walter Hooper, "is *That Hideous Strength*. It's sort of a fairy story set in modern times. It turns out to be many people's favorite book of Lewis's and his own too. He didn't think it was the best, but he told me he liked it the most."

"I think *Till We Have Faces* is probably the greatest work of fiction Jack ever wrote," said Gresham. "It is the retelling of the ancient myth of Cupid and Psyche—the story of a sister who marries a god and the sister who is left behind. It's a story of adventure, jealousy, love, despair, betrayal—all of those things. It is also a story of self-sacrifice, forgiveness, and reconciliation, which is, of course, the underlying Christian message. I've read it fifteen or sixteen times and I'm still finding new things within it. It was very badly received by critics when it was published, but now, it is a book that people are beginning to really understand and enjoy."

Was C. S. Lewis a misogynist?

"At no point does Lewis regard women as inferior to men," said Manlove. "A misogynist wouldn't have made women the center of his books in the way that he has. It's the women in *The Great Divorce* who are saved and who try to redeem the damned. It's Lucy who is the great perceiver in the Narnia books. The witch? All right, she's female, and much is made of that by one particular critic. In *Till We Have Faces* it is women who are at the center. There's a fallible woman in the form of Orual, but in the form of Psyche, whom Orual eventually becomes, is a woman redeemed."

"He was a typical male of that period," said Mitchell. "But I think it's a bit anachronistic, historically speaking, to call him a misogynist. He respected women. His treatment of Mrs. Moore and her daughter is an indication. Did he enjoy the company of women? Not for the most part. Is that a defect in his character? I think Lewis would have said yes, just as he would have said that not liking the company of small children is a defect in his character. Did he adhere to certain conceptions of the role a woman should play in society? Yes. Were those culturally informed? Many of them, yes. Was he a product of his age in that sense? Yes. But to say all that does not necessarily equate him to being a misogynist. Now, taken by today's standard, maybe yes, you could build a case. But things have changed dramatically."

"I've heard people say that he was not very gracious to women students," said Hart. "But I lived in England for twenty years and I met a number of women who had been at his lectures and his tutorials in Oxford. And they thought he was a wonderful tutor and that he listened to what his students said. And certainly when I met him for one afternoon, he was gracious and kind, and in no sense did he seem to be a know-it-all or arrogant."

Why do you think Americans are so receptive to Lewis's work?

"Americans have a Puritan tradition that is still very much alive," said Manlove. "I think that Americans are more able to live with their emotions. When I was in America, the one thing that struck me was how ready people were to talk about how they felt. One won't find that here [in the United Kingdom]. And I think that insofar as Lewis does that, that makes Americans very responsive. But he is ultimately attractive to Americans because of his conviction and because he is prepared to be scientific about it. I think American society looks quite vigorously for proofs of God's existence. People are not facile believers. They like to have their beliefs anchored in some kind of argument. And Lewis gives them that."

"I think the concept that C. S. Lewis's works are more popular in America than anywhere else is false," said Gresham. "There are readers from nations all around the world that are fascinated by Jack's works. What has really happened is that Americans are more ready to show their enthusiasm for such things than people in other countries. I mean, the British are renowned for not showing their enthusiasms or emotions, except, of course, when it comes to football. It is, however, probably true that Americans are more interested in matters of Christian spirituality than the British are at present.

"I think it's probably fair to say that the development of Christian thinking is based in the United States," continued Gresham. "I think America is leading the world in intellectual approaches to Christianity at the present time. And at the same time, it's only fair to say that America is also leading the world in the fields of sin and degradation as well. One of the things that I rather enjoy about America is the fact that it's a country of such huge contrasts spiritually and intellectually. And let's face it, Americans are getting awful sick of bull----. They've been fed it for too long and I think they are now searching for the truth. And so

I think C. S. Lewis's writings will become more popular in the States as people reach out for truth, simply told."

Do you think Lewis had a sense of his own greatness?

"I think he was very much aware that it was not he who was great," said Gresham. "Jack was very much aware that he was a conduit of the Holy Spirit of God and that that's where the greatness came from. That's where the wisdom came from. He certainly was aware of his intellectual abilities. He had a degree of intellectual vanity and was conscious of it and rueful of it. But I don't think he ever saw himself as being great. I think he attributed any greatness to the Holy Spirit, which is exactly where it belongs."

How would Lewis feel about the attention that is paid to his life and work?

"He didn't like this kind of thing," said Lyle Dorsett. "He wouldn't want people nosing into his past, or into Joy's past. He wouldn't want people trying to figure out whether he had an affair with Mrs. Moore. He wouldn't want people asking questions about whether he'd consummated the marriage with Joy. I think he would have found it amazing that anybody would think that they didn't. He would have found all this disgusting. But if I were sitting down and talking to him, I would say, 'You know, you can't write all the books you wrote and get your picture on the front of *Time* magazine and become so well known and think people aren't going to care. They just do. And maybe you don't think they should, but they do.' And I would have about as much sympathy for that point of view as I do for musicians and movie stars who find it tiresome."

"He became such a public figure while he eschewed that kind of thing," said Mitchell. "He never sought celebrity. His life was filled with friends, teaching at the college, walking. But he didn't take in the cinema. He didn't have a public social life. He wasn't on television. He was a man of habit. In contemporary American terms, he was a boring guy. His popularity really resides in his writings, the public profile of his writings, not him as a person."

Was he afraid of death?

"Oh no," said Gresham. "By the time he finally died, I think he was rather looking forward to it."

What do you think C. S. Lewis's legacy should be?

"Lewis was very much what he wrote," said Mitchell. "Everything he wrote had some evangelistic element involved. His passion was his faith, and to make it known on various levels. He did it in imaginative literature. He did it with apologetics. He was one of the most articulate Christians of the twentieth century. And if there's a legacy in terms of his Christianity, then that legacy is that he made it about as plausible as anybody did in that time period. At the end of the day you may not agree with him, but Christianity is no longer this sort of mindless beliefism. He believed that there's a reason for accepting these things and you can't just write it off. And those who do, I think, have not really listened to him."

Walter Hooper suggested, "In one way, he is a little world in himself. He left behind a huge body of work. I think it will be remembered because it is a huge picture of the world as a whole.

He provided not just a glimpse of truth, he really gave readers the big picture. While in other writers you get a corner of the curtain he's raised, you get a little bit of the truth, with Lewis the big curtains just open up wide and they extend all the way to the side of the theater and you see everything that is in front of you."

"Many, many lives have been utterly changed because of what he did," said Lyle Dorsett. "Broken people, wounded people, people bound up in all kinds of things they wanted to be free from, have found freedom through Jesus Christ whom Lewis pointed to. I was certainly one of those and I am not unique.

"In Ephesians, chapter 4," added Dorsett, "Paul wrote of the Spirit-ordained orders of ministry: Some are called to be apostles, some are called to be evangelists, some are called to be teachers. Lewis was a teacher. At the very core of who he was, he was a teacher."

"He knew what his apostolate was and he did it," said Hooper. "You might know what you're supposed to do in the world and you might not do it. But Lewis knew, and at great difficulty to himself, he did it."

"It's very easy to get fascinated by Jack's development as a human being, or to get fascinated by the development of his literature," concluded Douglas Gresham. "But all the time, no matter what the subjective angle of one's own interests are, we should look beyond that to the power of the Holy Spirit of God behind it, governing it, channeling it, guiding Jack all the time. That's what's really important. Jack himself is much less important."

A FINAL NOTE

*R*eaders should note that many of the locations that were important to C. S. Lewis can be visited in Oxford today. During our research and interviews for this book, we were pleased to find that locations such as the Trout restaurant still serve up a good meal; the Eagle and Child pub, which housed weekly meetings of the Inklings, is still a great spot to enjoy a stout on tap and view framed photos of Lewis and Tolkien; Magdalen College remains one of the most beautiful at Oxford University; the Kilns is now run by the C. S. Lewis Foundation; and the Holy Trinity Church and adjacent graveyard (where Lewis, Warnie, and Mrs. Moore are buried) is easily accessible in Headington Quarry. The

Cotswolds countryside near Oxford remains among the most beautiful locations in all of England for a quiet walk, an afternoon break for coffee or tea, or a peaceful drive.

For more information about the interviewers and author of this book, or the related television documentary, please visit the *DuncanEntertainment.com* Web site.

NOTES

INTRODUCTION

1. Perry Bramlett, "The Popularity of C. S. Lewis." 15 August 2001. <http://www.win.net/~pbramlett/Popularity/html>.

CHAPTER 1

1. C. S. Lewis, *Surprised by Joy: The Shape of My Early Life* (New York: Harcourt and Brace, 1955), 10.

2. Ibid., 21.

3. Ibid., 115.

4. Walter Hooper, ed., *They Stand Together: The Letters of C. S. Lewis to Arthur Greeves (1914–1916)* (New York: Macmillan, 1979), 135.

5. Walter Hooper, *C. S. Lewis: A Companion & Guide* (San Francisco: HarperSanFrancisco, 1996), 568.

6. Douglas Gilbert and Clyde Kilby, *C. S. Lewis: Images of His World* (Grand Rapids, Mich.: William B. Eerdmans, 1973), 9.

CHAPTER 2

1. Gilbert and Kilby, *C. S. Lewis: Images of His World,* 10.
2. Ibid.
3. Ibid., 11.
4. Ibid., 10–11.
5. Ibid., 11.

CHAPTER 3

1. Gilbert and Kilby, *C. S. Lewis: Images of His World,* 12.
2. Lewis, *Surprised by Joy,* 191.
3. C. S. Lewis, *God in the Dock: Essays on Theology and Ethics,* ed. Walter Hooper (Grand Rapids, Mich.: William B. Eerdmans, 1970, 1999), 66–67.
4. Ibid., 67.
5. Wayne Martindale and Jerry Root, eds., *The Quotable Lewis* (Wheaton, Ill.: Tyndale House Publishers, 1989), 356.
6. Lewis, *Surprised by Joy,* 17–18.
7. C. S. Lewis, *The Lion, the Witch and the Wardrobe: A Story for Children* (New York: HarperCollins, 1994), 68.
8. Martindale and Root, *The Quotable Lewis,* 354.

CHAPTER 4

1. C. S. Lewis, *The Problem of Pain* (New York: HarperCollins, 2001), 90–91.

CHAPTER 5

1. C. S. Lewis, *The Screwtape Letters with Screwtape Proposes a Toast* (New York: HarperCollins, 2001), 25.
2. Ibid., 93.

CHAPTER 6

1. C. S. Lewis, *Mere Christianity* (New York: HarperCollins, 2001), viii.
2. Ibid., ix.
3. Ibid., 54, 55.

CHAPTER 7

1. George Sayer, *Jack: A Life of C. S. Lewis* (Wheaton, Ill.: Crossway Books, 1994), 317.
2. Jackie Loohaus, "Hobbit forming: Tolkien continues to set readers' imaginations to work." 9 June 2000. <http://www.jsonline.com/enter/books/jun00/tolk11060900.asp>.

CHAPTER 9

1. Hooper, *C. S. Lewis: A Companion & Guide*, 100.

CHAPTER 10

1. C. S. Lewis, *A Grief Observed* (San Francisco: Harper & Row, 1989), 48.
2. Ibid., 73.

CHAPTER 11

1. Sayer, *Jack,* 410.

Photographs
and Illustrations

92
LEW

14079

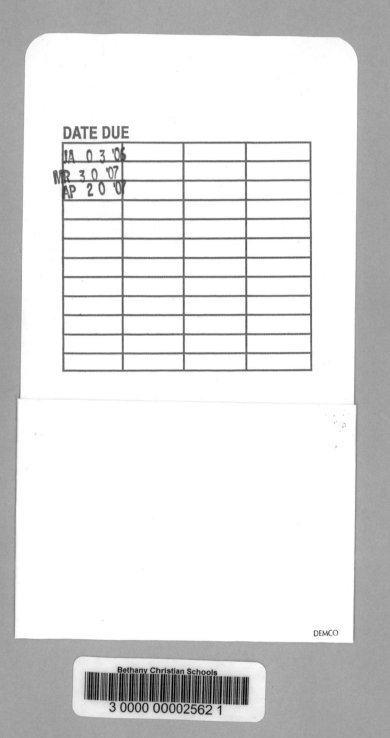

DATE DUE

JA 0 3 '06			
MR 3 0 '07			
AP 2 0 '07			

DEMCO